Praise for
The Hybrid Sales Channel

The Hybrid Sales Channel is a conversation starter for organizations interested in aligning sales paradigms with how customers buy and creating a shared vision for organic growth. Through a mix of storytelling, actionable concepts, and thoughtful illumination of all sides of the vendor-partner-customer dynamic, Rich quickly and succinctly lays out a roadmap for success. This isn't your ordinary journey. Be prepared to walk away eager to solve some very interesting sales challenges and untangle relationships between direct and channel sales to foster organic, long-term growth.

—Heather K. Margolis, founder and President,
Channel Maven Consulting

In his book Rich tackles today's big routes-to-market question: What is and how do you manage a hybrid sales channel? This book is a must for both traditional channel and direct sales leaders, offering real-life insights and practical advice on how to minimize conflict. Importantly, Rich reminds us that the key question should be not which route or routes to market are best for you, but which will most effectively serve the needs of your customers and prospective customers.

—Rod Baptie, President, Baptie & Company Ltd.

Plain and simple, sales leaders succeed by producing organic revenue growth. This is a versatile and highly sensible guide to driving organic revenue growth by fully utilizing the talent, relationships, product, and overall strength of both internal sales professionals and channel partners. Rich tells a story and illustrates a playbook for getting the most out of direct and indirect channels by closing the gaps between them and in turn, maximizing organic growth. I will put these practices in place immediately in my own sales organization. Thanks, Rich!

—Lane Brannan, SVP Global Sales, Four Winds Interactive

In *The Hybrid Sales Channel*, Rich Blakeman has laid out a very thoughtful and succinct approach to maximizing growth. With such fundamental tenets as keeping the customer at the center of what you do, understanding the customer will buy the way they want to buy and not the way you want to sell, realizing nobody "owns" the customer, and connecting with the customer by aligning your sales process to their buying process, Rich has done a brilliant job of leveraging all sales channels through a singular, customer centric, approach. A must-read for all people looking to optimize their distribution channels.

—Bob Picinich, SVP of Sales Effectiveness (retired),
Global U.S.-based insurance firm

The Hybrid Sales Channel takes us on a trip to a promising land of rich possibilities. The book is part Broadway play, part sales strategy playbook, and part time-tested sales bible that offers many profitable "aha" moments that will lead sales executives to explore the many benefits of a hybrid sales channel strategy. The good news is that MHI Global is the leader in this growing field and Rich is their top thought leader on the subject. Rich is not only a superb storyteller, but he also makes a very convincing case for embracing the new model that can help you create far more customers.

—Gerhard Gschwandtner, Publisher, *Selling Power*

Nothing in business starts until somebody sells something. Focusing on igniting sales should be the challenge of the day every day—a challenge shared by every member of a customer-focused company that wants to be world-class. Rich has spent the time to listen, to learn, and to lead change. He has the knowledge and the heart to make you outrageously successful.

—David Richard, VP of Global Services,
North America (retired), IBM Corporation

Most organizations claim to be "customer centric," but in reality they are merely paying lip service to the philosophy. Customer 3.0 has arrived and any company who does not place them at the center of their universe will allow the competition to thrive.

Rich Blakeman doesn't just discuss how critical it is to have round pegs in round holes; he also provides a superb comprehensive route map. The very best sales professionals are now specialists—the days of the "generalist" are numbered and soon they will be consigned to the annals of history. This is a must-read for anyone who wishes to not only survive but who has a desire to thrive.

—Jonathan Farrington, CEO, *Top Sales World*

The Hybrid Sales Channel is crisp and on target regarding the misstep of working to maximize both direct and indirect sales channels separately, versus in concert. While change will be met with fear and resistance, Blakeman outlines paths that can help in a "back of a napkin" approach—while at the same time providing the road map and tools to take it to execution and results.

—Robert M. Peterson, PhD, White Lodging
Professor of Sales, Northern Illinois University

When Miller Heiman, Inc. bought the Australian company Channel Enablers several years ago, I had no idea what the company did or why MHI bought them because I was not involved in the decision to buy the company. I admit it. I was a total ignoramus. In other words, "I simply did not know what I did not know." I was in a fog because of lack of knowledge. When one lacks knowledge, one is ignorant. And indeed I was.

What Rich Blakeman has accomplished brilliantly with his new book, *The Hybrid Sales Channel,* is to articulate precisely and concisely what a so-called hybrid sales channel is and further gives a detailed how-to to effectively thrive and successfully sell through this somewhat mysterious channel. The book is very user-friendly and readable, clear, and to the point. In short, it is an excellent "read."

Further, Blakeman then shows exactly how to adapt the Miller Heiman sales tools, proven effective for over 40 years in B2B, B2C, OEM, and other channels, along with the best of current thinking of indirect channel sales—so that there may be consistency of sales approach among the various sales channels in any sales organization.

This book is highly recommended reading for both the neophyte to the hybrid sales channel and those like me who want to just reduce their ignoramus quotient.

—Robert B. "Bob" Miller, founder, Miller Heiman, Inc.

The
Hybrid Sales Channel

The
Hybrid Sales Channel

How to Ignite Growth by Bridging the Gap Between Direct and Indirect Sales

By Rich Blakeman

New York Chicago San Francisco Athens London Madrid
Mexico City Milan New Delhi Singapore Sydney Toronto

1 2 3 4 5 6 7 8 9 0 DOC/DOC 1 2 1 0 9 8 7 6 5

ISBN   978-0-07-184532-8
MHID   0-07-184532-1

e-ISBN   978-0-07-184533-5
e-MHID   0-07-184533-X

Library of Congress Cataloging-in-Publication Data

Blakeman, Rich
    The hybrid sales channel : how to ignite growth by bridging the gap
  between direct and indirect sales / Rich Blakeman.
        pages cm
     ISBN 978-0-07-184532-8 (alk. paper)—ISBN 0-07-184532-1 (alk. paper)
  1. Sales management.   2. Direct selling.   3. Marketing channels.
  I. Title.
     HF5438.4.B596 2016
     658.8'7—dc23   2015029328

McGraw-Hill Education books are available at special quantity discounts to use as premiums and sales promotions or for use in corporate training programs. To contact a representative, please visit the Contact Us pages at www.mhprofessional.com.

This book is dedicated to all of those who struggle to deal with the effects of Alzheimer's disease:

- For those who suffer from the disease, may their journey be eased
- For their loved ones who cannot possibly walk a mile in their shoes, yet care so deeply to make their remaining years meaningful and easier to journey through
- For their thankless caregivers, who put up with and give so much, and often get so little in return
- For those researching and studying the disease, its cause, and its effects—whose work cannot come to fruition fast enough
- For the millions of individuals, organizations, and corporations who fund the effort to understand and eradicate this indiscriminate, horrible disease

And to my mother, Anne Fox Blakeman,
July 25, 1925–October 22, 2001.
I love you, Mom.

Contents

Foreword

Why This? Why Now?

When Rich came to me to share the concepts of this book and ask me to write the foreword, I was about three months into my new role as the leader of MHI Global. I had a lot on my mind at the time, bringing together some of the world's greatest brands in our industry in order to serve our clients better and help them sell more, more profitably. The very first questions we engaged on were just these: Why this? Why now?

It wasn't a very long conversation. Just as, so I'm told, it wasn't a very long conversation between Rich and the editorial staff at McGraw-Hill when he presented the book concept to them originally. Maybe the shortest sales cycle of his career!

There has been an absolute shift in our profession—the profession of sales. We've stopped talking about ourselves—how we sell, how we pitch, how we close—and we have moved the entire conversation to being about the customer.

If you know nothing else about our MHI Global team, know that our most important belief is this:

The most important decision we make as salespeople, managers, and leaders is how to connect with our customers.

We have layers and years of research that back up the fact that the companies that do this best and most often win more and more profitably. Hopefully, this isn't new news to you, even if it isn't yet at the top of your strategic sales initiatives.

How does this play into my two questions? Simple. With the shift in our profession comes one irrefutable truth: We can decide all we'd like about how we want to *sell*, but in the end, the customer is going to decide how they want to *buy*. I can't state the case for this book more simply than that—customers are deciding, every day, that our traditional sales models do not suit them. They don't care why we separate direct from indirect sales to fit our own cost economics—and they don't like it when we try to tell them how we want them to buy from us. That truth is driving a higher and higher percentage of customer spending through partners and less through our historically esteemed and deeply qualified direct sales channels.

We have to adapt to the market and do it quickly. Each in our own way, based on the markets and customers we serve.

And we have to do it now. Why now? Two simple reasons: (1) If you don't, someone else already is, and (2) growth, in every one of our companies, is no longer an option—it's required; not creating growth makes for a very short shelf life as a sales leader.

The notion of a hybrid sales channel is not new—companies have had some version of hybrid territories or market coverage in place for years. Territory sales professionals have forged relationships with their distributors, resellers, agents, or other business partners and worked in some form of teaming fashion or another. What I've seen, however, is a high degree of variation—in design, execution, and results. This is another set of characteristics that leads to a short shelf life.

Why this, and why now?

- We know that we can no longer get by on talent alone. A scalable, consistent selling methodology is everything. Market conditions are causing us to morph to a hybrid approach, yet a formal model didn't exist—until *The Hybrid Sales Channel.*

- We know that customers are looking for perspective, not a pitch. In order to provide perspective, we have to make sure that we have the right people aligned with the right customers in the buying process. These sales professionals bring the necessary perspective to influence how *this* group of people will make *this* decision, *this* time. To do this right in today's conditions will almost always require one form of a hybrid sales channel or another.

- We know that the best are always looking for ways to improve. We know this experientially from the clients we work with at MHI Global, but more importantly, our research drives this home as fact. World-class sales teams know what their top performers do to create their results, and they know how to share and replicate top performance behaviors across their organization. In the world of blending direct and indirect sales teams to ignite growth, we'll shorten that cycle for you.

- Finally, we know that those who prepare, win more and win more consistently. The more time a customer spends with you, the more value they expect you to deliver—and you can only deliver value in a repeatable way by preparing and then executing. The gap between world class and all other sales professionals in this area is distressing. Here's a simple highlight from our 2015 research, the *2015 MHI Sales Best Practices Study*: 82 percent of world-class sales performers say that they clearly understand their customers' issues before they propose a solution—while only 34 percent of all others can make the same statement. Scary for our profession. This book is nothing if not about preparation and execution.

We're at a tipping point. More people are involved in buying decisions than ever before (averaging 5.8 people per buying decision based on our *2015 MHI Sales Best Practices Study* for world-class performers). We have more people involved in every sale than ever before (4.4 per sale), sales cycles are getting longer (up another 2.8 percent this last year), and more customers have formalized their buying process and are expecting return on investment (ROI) calculations before making purchasing decisions. More is expected of us, and we must deliver more.

That's why this book and why now. I hope you enjoy the read, but more importantly, I hope it helps you engage and connect with your customers and bring them more value.

—Byron Matthews, President and
General Manager, MHI Global

Acknowledgments

I suppose like any other first-time author, there is a risk that my chronicle of the people I am in debt to will exceed readers' attention spans. That said, I am deeply indebted to:

- My early IBM mentors, colleagues, and leaders— from Indianapolis to Minneapolis and everywhere in between—who taught me what it meant to put people and customers first. And especially to David Richard, who had the confidence in me to give me several leadership opportunities on his team, and after leaving IBM pulled me in again to join his team at Norstan. David taught me what it meant to lead.
- All of my clients around the world for more than 35 years who have afforded me the opportunity to understand their businesses and attempt to help them get better.
- The two people who inspired me the most over my last nine years at MHI Global: the one and only Bob Miller, for always holding me accountable to what is important,

and Sam Reese, who brought me into this business at the tipping point of change.

- The founders, leaders, and consultants of Channel Enablers, the consultancy we acquired in 2011 and that I have been blessed with the opportunity to lead. Specifically, Braham Shnider, Geoff Wright, and Phil Moon—who accepted me into their family and welcomed me as one of their own. You are amazing partners.

- The dozens of books on my bookshelf written by personal friends, which both shamed and inspired me to arrive late to their party. I hope you find me worthy of joining the club.

- My two editing and writing co-conspirators: Melissa Paulik, without whose brilliance, guidance, and counsel I would still be wandering in the wilderness; and Donya Dickerson at McGraw-Hill, who said yes to the concept after a 20-minute phone call—and then had the drive, ambition, and guts to stick it out with me through every step of the way.

- My father, Ray Blakeman, and my father-in-law, Ron Betters—businessmen worthy of admiration and accolade, yet as humble as any you will ever meet. Choices and consequences, the stuff life is made of.

* And more than the sum of all above, the bedrock of my
family: my wife, Tammy; daughter, Wendy; and son,
David—for encouraging me to be myself, and always
wanting me to be the best I can be for all of us. I love
you all.

Introduction

*A Hybrid Sales Channel—Just Exactly
What Do You Mean by That?*

W*hat do you mean by a hybrid sales channel?* This is the most frequent question I've received while writing this book. That's not surprising. In my role as the Managing Director of MHI Global's Channel Sales Center of Excellence, I've talked to companies across industries and geographies around the world—and their interpretations of the term are as wide and varied as the companies themselves. Here's a small sample of what I've heard:

- *We have a hybrid sales channel. Our direct sales team sells to the end customer, and our distributors fulfill every sale. We have no sales that are not channel sales— hybrid channel sales between direct and indirect.*
- *We have a different hybrid between direct sales and indirect sales in every market. In mature markets, our direct reps sell only enterprise accounts while our channel partners sell all other segments. In emerging*

markets, we sell 100 percent through distribution and have no direct sales at all. Our entire company is made up of a hybrid of sales channels.

- *We work hard to keep our direct sales channel and our indirect sales channel completely separate and distinct from one another—by market segment, customer, or other variables—to make sure we have no duplication of cost. The only time we end up with what you might call a "hybrid" is when the customer forces us into it by how they want to buy, not because of how we want to sell.*

Surely there are a dozen other permutations and combinations of each of these discussions, but the point is clear—there is no clarity on what it means to have a hybrid sales channel.

Let's start with the premise made by the last example: *"The only time we end up with what you might call a 'hybrid' is when the customer forces us into it by how they want to buy, not because of how we want to sell."* As ludicrous as it sounds in today's market-driven economy, whether stated or unstated, this is the position of many companies around the world today. It is true whether you observe their organizational structure, strategy, tactics, or actions in the marketplace. Companies have fooled themselves into believing they can influence or dictate how customers will buy, and they follow that supposition through to designing go-to-market approaches that reflect how they want to sell rather than how customers want to buy.

Hopefully, you've chosen to read this book for some reason other than to rationalize or reinforce your current thinking and strategy. Perhaps you're enamored by the subtitle of the book and want to understand what is meant by *igniting growth through the intersection of direct and indirect sales*. I imagine you're especially focused on those words "igniting growth."

If you were inspired by Byron's foreword, *Why This, Why Now?*, the combination of igniting growth and the immediacy of the "now" requires us to be very specific in defining what we mean by a hybrid sales channel.

There are some wonderful parallels across disciplines that get to the key point of promise of this book. Let's begin in the world of biology. Why do farmers or winemakers work so hard to cross-breed different strains of their crops to form all sorts of varieties and *hybrids* of vegetables or grapes? In most cases they are seeking to make the resulting hybrid:

- Taste better than other products to the consumer
- Create a better yield or production
- Be more resistant to disease or other factors that prevent perfection in growing the perfect produce

- Become part of a more competitive or tasty blend with other produce or elements that go into a broader recipe or end product

The factors that drive hybrid production in farming are nearly all market driven, not product driven or technology driven. The growers want to make the best, most differentiated products for consumers to consume. It isn't about having the coolest genetics or the cleverest packaging.

The parallels here are almost too obvious when thinking about direct and indirect sales, so let's move on to another parallel—the hybrid car industry. What factors created the hybrid car industry, and how did it "come together"? The earliest history of hybrid cars begins with Dr. Ferdinand Porsche in the late 1800s, but the most instructive history begins with the mass-produced models of Toyota and Honda delivered beginning in the late 1990s. Again, what factors caused these global leaders to create a hybrid vehicle in the face of the tremendous success of their gasoline-powered existing technology?

- Increasing consumer cost of gasoline
- Government pressure on emission control
- Government subsidies for consumers investing in alternative energies
- Marketing buzz around the beginnings of an eco-friendly, "green" consumer base

Other than the common thread between hybrid crops and cars being a market-driven basis, the hybrid car provides a deeper parallel to set the example for a hybrid sales channel. What is at the core of the design of a hybrid automobile?

They have two engines, one gas and one electric, each one maximized to its own potential and doing what it does best. One feeds off the other, both working together to achieve the common goal: efficient output and resource use.

As we'll develop, this is at the core of what a hybrid sales channel is. But, let's not get ahead of ourselves. The core take-away concepts from the hybrid car are simple:

- The gas engine and the electric motor are separate but co-dependent. The hybrid car would not function without both of them working in concert.
- Each engine has specific characteristics that make it best suited for certain tasks and a computer that ensures that the right engine is engaged to do the right task at the right time—and ensures that the other engine is not doing the same task at the same time.
- The gasoline engine can in fact charge the energy level of the electric motor. A third system, the braking system, can also charge the batteries that

drive the electric motor. All of the systems work together, not separately.

The Hybrid Sales Channel was conceived and is built with these concepts in mind. The end goal is to provide a differentiated experience for end customers that causes them to buy more of your products and services than those of your competitors. The core question is: How do you build and manage a coverage model that maximizes every aspect of your direct and indirect resources to drive maximum growth in a marketplace where the customers get to choose how they buy? Our history as a profession is fairly predictable and mostly the opposite: designing elegant cost structures and routes to markets that reflect how we want to sell.

I can hear the skeptics already:

- *It won't work. We've tried this before. The channel isn't ready.*
- *It won't work. The customer depends on our direct sales team being the thought leaders for them—we can't position the channel to take that spot.*
- *We've spent too much time separating our cost structures and building rules of engagement to drive the differences between our direct and indirect routes. It would be madness to undo all of that and build some kind of hybrid.*

And the list goes on. The skeptics have a problem for every solution. My wife would have me borrow a phrase from Dr. Phil at this point: "How's that working for you?"

There's no question that revenue growth through the channel is on the rise in almost every industry and geography around the world, but that's happening because of how customers want to buy, not because of how we want to sell. The questions we don't want to answer are much harder: How is our total share of customer wallet growing, between our direct and our channels? How are we doing with absolute new organic growth in revenue and margin contribution, removing any acquisition growth? How are *those* working with our current coverage model?

We need to learn the lesson of the hybrid car: two engines with different purposes, both working together, neither duplicating what the other does at any time, one charging the other when it needs it. Let's get to work.

CHAPTER ONE

A Story of a Hybrid Sales Channel—How It All Began

Act One: It All Started on a Cocktail Napkin

All good sales stories do, don't they?

In this case, it began with a sales manager and one of her direct sales reps, sitting at the Altitude Bar in Singapore. The manager calmly looked out from the highest point in the city, while the sales rep was fretting over the largest quota he'd ever been given—$7 million!

John had made his number every year for the past five years, but Jasmine was new to the company and new to this industry segment. John had seen plenty of managers come and go during his days, but he wasn't sure about this one. His peers had told him there was something different about her so John had his "new boss" antennae turned on. Jasmine, on the other hand, had meticulously planned this discussion and rehearsed it over and over—with her boss, and subsequently in her mind—until she was certain she was ready.

Jasmine pulled out a pen and reached for a cocktail napkin. John calmed in a flash. There was nothing she could do to outsell him on a cocktail napkin! Jasmine drew a circle in the middle of the napkin and wrote "$7M" above the circle.

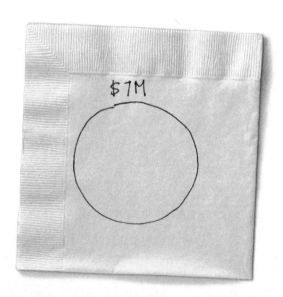

"John, how do you feel about your quota for this year?"

Feel? The antennae went on high alert. Surely she didn't want to know how he really felt right now. All of the normal emotions flew through him:

- I pulled the first half of this year into last year. You must be crazy!
- I sold everything there was to sell and my largest client is about to be acquired. I'm looking for a lower quota, not a higher one!
- You just got here. You don't know me, my customers, my territory, or the industry segment. I'm guessing you all just threw darts over at the Boomerang the other night and my quota came up seven!

But instead of blurting out any of these responses and despite the loud pinging of his antennae, John was a professional to the max: "It's a stretch for sure, Jasmine, but I'm sure we can make it if we put together the right plan early on."

At that point, Jasmine knew she had John. She knew she could win him over to the number she had already committed to her vice president. She smiled and nodded, "John, I couldn't agree more with you." She picked her pen back up and continued drawing on the napkin.

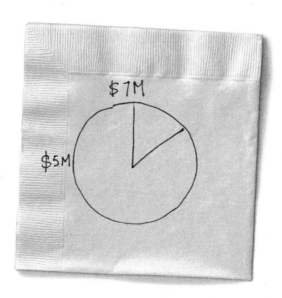

"How would you feel if I told you that I only want you to personally focus on and close $5 million of the $7 million of your quota? A million less than you did last year and $2 million less than the whole seven?"

As you can imagine, John's radar went off like a storm warning. Is this what everyone meant by "there's something different about her"? John wanted to react with his normal smart-mouthed, "NOW we're talking, baby!" But he chose the high road. He knew there had to be more to this story.

"I'm listening. . . ."

The conversation continued long into the Singapore night, and the cocktail napkin got more complicated the longer they talked—to the point where the average person looking at it would have no idea what they had been discussing. John and Jasmine took turns picking up the pen to elaborate and expand on her basic concept. At the end of the evening (and truth be told, a few $16 cocktails later that didn't end up on the expense account), John looked Jasmine straight in the eye and extended his hand, "You've got yourself a deal! How do we get started?"

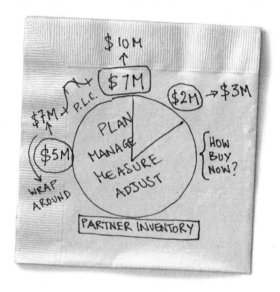

The crux of this conversation is happening across dozens of industries today: How do you take your highest-cost, highest-value resource—the vendor's experienced direct outside sales rep—and focus that person on the business he or she is best suited to cover and close . . . all while still growing accounts, industries, and territories faster and deeper than any one sales rep can cover alone?

It's not just sales leaders in complex, dynamic industries like technology and telecommunications having these discussions. You can look at Halliburton's low-tech business of selling the lubricating "mud" used in drilling and mining—a business where the customers are so dependent on the red hard-hatted Halliburton sales reps as the absolute subject matter experts that it risks tying growth solely to the ability to either add more high-cost direct sales professionals . . . or find a way to adopt Jasmine and John's cocktail napkin.

So what did all of that scribbling on the napkin mean? What caused the grizzly veteran to turn 180 degrees and buy into Jasmine's plan? What was Jasmine's plan from the start? The answer to those questions, and to John's most important question—"How do we get started?"—is the subject of this book. Let's be clear about what *The Hybrid Sales Channel* is and what it is not before we hear Jasmine explain some of the concepts in her own words.

The Hybrid Sales Channel is:

- An approach to growing top-line sales organically and exponentially faster than staying the course of a current direct sales approach
- A systematic way of identifying how your end customers are buying today, how they want to buy (both your

products and complementary ones), and facilitating what those customers *are already choosing to do*

- Practice, not theory, about how direct sales reps can involve the *right* business partners, in the *right* parts of their accounts or territories, working with the *right* contacts and buying influences—to drive more sales, better sales, faster sales
- The management approach and metrics for making it *work* and making it stick

The Hybrid Sales Channel is *not*:

- A focused analysis of cost-based sales models, aimed at the bottom line. This is a discussion about growing the top line, not competing or complementary models of sales cost of different routes to market.
- A solution to resolve conflict over compensation between channels. There are as many successes as failures on this road already. These failures are most often driven by the desire to minimize cost, *not maximize growth!* As the principles of a hybrid sales channel evolve into execution and become successful, the idea is to drive enough incremental top-line revenue growth to fund the model. Each successful growth company always finds the right way to compensate success.

- A primer on how to migrate accounts currently covered by direct sales "over to the channel." There is enough history already written on what works here (and much more unwritten about what does not work).
- An approach aimed primarily at the channel management profession. Channel managers are tasked with driving the overall efficiency and effectiveness (and productivity!) of the whole of their channel partners. This book is aimed at the efficiency and effectiveness of individual sales and support professionals *within* a partner firm when they are correctly engaged by the *right* direct sales rep for the *right* reasons.

Act Two: It Actually Began in the Boardroom

While all good sales stories may start on a cocktail napkin, all true business stories begin in the boardroom. It could have been any boardroom, anywhere. The CEO and CFO sitting by themselves, exhausted from the board meeting that followed the analyst's call. The pressure had been more intense than usual for a non-quarter-ending meeting, and while they felt the need to decompress, there was no time to take a breath.

The message had been clear: *You have cut costs to make your numbers for far too many quarters in a row while promising to deliver on growth.*

And the antecedent message: *Given your debt-to-equity posture and current market capitalization, there's no way to acquire yourself to growth. You haven't shown the accretive growth and integration benefits yet from the acquisitions you've made over the past three years.*

It's time to produce true incremental organic growth.

A sobering message to be sure, and one that demands action. Looking only at the rewards of having a "C-Suite" job, the public misses these kinds of footnotes in a financial statement. Risk and reward go hand and hand, and the company was either traveling on the tip of the spear or was going to have to guide the arrow to the bullseye while driving from the feathers.

I've met many global heads of sales who aspire to that fabled "C-Suite" job. On days like these, however, they're not envious of never being invited to present to the analysts or directly to the board.

Why is that, by the way? If analysts are chirping about organic growth, then why not regularly hear from sales leadership directly during analyst calls? The reasons are simple, sound, and specific:

1. Typically one or both of two signatures of corporate officers are on every financial disclosure and reporting document required by any regulatory body: the CEO and the CFO. The analysts want to hear from those

who are directly accountable for setting expectations and then living up to them.

2. That said, these are the officers that analysts and the board have come to know and trust. If sales data are to be presented, outlooks to be given, or perspectives shared on the results of executing any corporate strategy that sales is tasked with carrying out, the CEO or CFO will present it.

3. Finally, let's be honest with ourselves: As a profession we've not always been the most predictable performers on the planet. If you graphed performance versus forecast quarter over quarter over the long run, there is reasonable evidence to support why many CFOs edit sales-generated data before the data go to the board or into financial reports.

Regardless of the history, track record, or data, the message coming out of this board meeting was clear: *Grow organically. Now.*

Dominique, CEO for the past four years, broke the silence between her CFO, Jorge, by walking to the whiteboard. To start the conversation that had been brewing in her mind since the middle of the board meeting, she scrawled some simple, direct observations:

On the whiteboard next to the first, she sketched out the following:

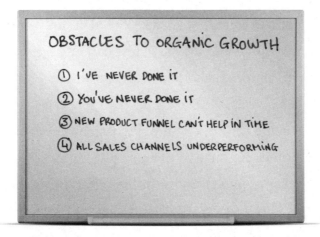

Jorge sat quietly, taken aback at first by how quickly Dominique had called the two of them out on their lack of history in growing companies organically. Dominique was always first to the bell when it came to personal accountability, but this was a new level of self-disclosure, *and she was right.* The two of them had worked together in two firms prior to this one and, in both cases, had fantastic track records with growth that had brought them together again here. *But it had all been growth through acquisition and integration leverage.*

That portion of the ensuing conversation didn't last long. "Facts are facts," as Dominique was fond of saying. Neither did the discussion regarding the new product funnel. Although there were some great innovations in the product line ahead, none of them could provide the kind of results that the board needed in the time that was expected. The first substantive question that Jorge asked was: "How can our sales channels' lack of performance be both an obstacle and an opportunity, Dominique?"

This became the crux of the discussion that caused them to order dinner in, instead of their normal routine of having their spouses join them for dinner after a board meeting. Dominique was very clear in her depiction of what she saw, and she saw it from the end customer's perspective.

"Jorge, it's not so much *that* our sales channels are underperforming. It's *why*. I've met with a half-dozen of our customer CEOs in the past month, and they all tell the same story. The way they are buying is changing, and we need to change the way we are going to market to match.

"Let's take some of our software offerings as the best example. Our enterprise teams, as well as our channel partners, have been selling them primarily through different functions of the customer's CIO organization for 20 years. Oh, they'll tell us that they have great relationships with all of the appropriate functional areas of the business, but our customers tell me that where they see us present is in IT."

The message from the end customers couldn't have been clearer. With the advent of the cloud and other software delivery models, the end-user executives were being allocated more and more budget that had previously been IT spend. "And," Dominique pointed out, "we are not present, or not *effectively* present, in those conversations. Not us, nor any of our chosen business partners in the market."

A half-dozen more examples and scenarios bounced back and forth between them until the whiteboard became a scribbled mess. The alignment between Dominique and Jorge grew more and more solid as the evening progressed. Eventually, they created a short list of must-do's that would form the beginning of their approach:

* Cover the market from the perspective of how the customer buys, not how we want to sell.

- Align the right resources from all sales channels to the right selling opportunities and selling actions, without duplication of effort.
- Remove the competition and confusion between the company's routes to market, especially those that are rooted in maximizing the individual wealth of our own employees.

Jorge found it easy to align around the simplicity and clarity of Dominique's perspective: sell more, sell more efficiently, and sell in ways that are aligned with how the customer wants to buy. However, he reserved his primary professional objection, the one he was struggling with the most, until he was sure there was complete alignment between himself and Dominique on the key principles of their plan. He knew he'd get a call in the morning from the chair of the board's finance committee asking about reactions to today's meeting and the plan to move forward to the "meet the organic growth" objective. It was the last of Dominique's whiteboard items—*focus on growth, not costs*—that scared him the most when thinking about that call.

"Dominique, we've done a great job with taking cost out of the business. The board said so today, even while they were chastising us over the lack of organic growth. How can we face them and say that we are going to tackle *this* problem by focusing on growth without focusing on cost? Is that truly what you mean?"

Dominique smiled, knowing that Jorge would cringe the moment she had written it. Indeed, she had written it very purposefully—and equally purposefully, had written it last.

"I mean it as a guiding principle for sure, my friend. I don't yet know, until we get some others involved, how exactly things will turn out from a cost perspective when we focus first on growth, but I do know this: our maniacal focus on the cost of each sales channel, direct and indirect, and our ability to keep ourselves balanced internally so that costs are in line with returns has gotten us to where we are today. We're going to have to do some things differently to get different results."

Dominique reached for her mobile phone, calling Henri, her global EVP of sales. The conversation was fast and furious, as Dominique got straight to the point. Dominique, Henri, and Jorge would meet the next afternoon at 5:00 p.m.—and Dominique expected Henri to come to the meeting with some concepts that would take the whiteboard principles to a level of execution that could get them to growth.

"That woke him up. See you tomorrow, Jorge."

Act Three: The Challenge to the Sales Leader

At best, Henri, Dominique's global EVP of sales, had a restless night's sleep. On the spur of the moment, he found himself having to process the boardroom direction and come up with a strategy and set of tactics. The message had been urgent and clear, which made it all the more important that his morning recommendations and questions be equally so. A few key words had struck Henri from the brief phone call: *organic growth, market coverage, customer centric.* Although Dominique hadn't said it outright, it was clear that change wasn't optional.

Henri thought through how this same phone call might have been received by each of his regional sales leaders and his global head of channel sales. Each would have reacted differently, he suspected, based on the challenges in their own marketplaces and geography. Looking at the challenge through a direct versus indirect lens made it harder to get clarity, not easier. There had to be a different answer, one that leveraged all of the possible resources available inside and outside the company—an answer that represented true change that could and would stick and create organic growth.

Henri sketched out his thoughts early in the morning. The key to his restless night had been one central theme: How do I leverage both my direct and my indirect resources in a coherent, planned, noncompetitive, and nonoverlapping coverage strategy? The word "hybrid" didn't immediately occur to Henri, and honestly, a blended or combined channel approach wasn't Henri's first or natural reaction. Like most sales leaders, he had spent his career working to maximize both direct and indirect sales channels separately, not together. He was proud of his ability to drive the right products through the right channel into the right market at the right cost and avoid (for the most part) duplicating cost wherever possible.

Part of his restless night caused by the odd messaging from Dominique had been knowing that it was also coming from Jorge. Focus on growth, not on cost? That wasn't Jorge's mantra, ever! More than once Henri had been the recipient of an income statement with red notations from Jorge asking how he could slash the expense line called "partner commissions." It had taken Henri several iterations to rid Jorge of the idea that partner sales expense could be reduced without any risk to revenue. Jorge had viewed it as expense alone, not as revenue generation through a channel. Over time, Henri had finally helped him understand that every dollar of partner expense came with partner-generated revenue—and that turning that knob up or down had the same effect on both numbers.

Yet now, this duet coming from the boardroom suggested that growth was more important than cost, market coverage was more important than channel separation, and maximizing the value of both the direct sales force *and* the channel partners' sales resources had to be accomplished to drive higher cross-sale penetration rates and more significant new account acquisition.

No wonder Henri didn't sleep much that night. In the morning, he started with some principles on his own whiteboard that would guide his thinking. We've seen some of these already in the work that Jasmine laid out with John.

- DIVIDE AND CONQUER IN DIRECT TERRITORIES
- FOCUS DIRECT REPS WHERE THEY HAVE UNIQUE STRENGTHS
- ALIGN PARTNER REPS TO THEIR GREATEST VALUE
- DON'T TURN DIRECT REPS INTO CHANNEL MANAGERS!

Henri was certain he could develop these key tenets to support the strategies that Dominique had outlined. His biggest concern was the last bullet: If he was going to lead the company through a game-changing coverage approach, this might be the largest change management challenge of his career. His direct teams were bred to be control freaks, and he was going to need to figure out how to leverage them *and* partner sales reps in the same territories without losing productivity. More to the point, he needed to show them how they could be more productive!

Henri knew he would need a systematic approach to offset the objections that would arise *from both direct and indirect sales leadership* when the notion of hybrid coverage was proposed:

* How do we keep the direct team focused on driving the revenue we need them to drive if they are also mapping and managing their territory for the hybrid channel?
* Isn't creating this kind of coverage strategy the job of the channel managers? Shouldn't they be doing this already with every partner account? Why distract the direct sales force and make their jobs more complex than they already are?
* If you're telling me that the partners are already selling into our direct accounts and that customers are going to buy however they choose to buy, why do we need to build some kind of a complex hybrid system that may put all of our channels at risk?

Like any change, these objections are founded in the two core elements of the basic issue: fear and a lack of information. Henri sketched out a flow that he thought might make sense at all levels of the organization:

In order to clarify and simplify his ideas about a breakthrough coverage model, Henri had to get down to role delineation. Simply stated, Henri had no intent, design, or desire to build a hybrid sales channel that would turn direct reps into channel managers.

Channel managers, as depicted in the right two boxes of Henri's diagram, serve an incredibly important function by working on two levels:

- At the market strategy level, they focus on:
  1. The overall market mapping and coverage strategy to ensure the right number and type of partners.
  2. Making sure the right programs and enablement are in place across all partners.

3. The right mix of routes to market to achieve the desired sales results.

- At the individual partner organization level, they:

1. Usually work with the owners, principals, and leadership of the partner firm.

2. Ensure the right resources, enablement, compensation, alignment, metrics, and all other aspects of strong joint partnership are in place to meet both their company's objectives and the partner's company objectives.

Channel managers did not, for the most part, get involved in the selling and account-level activities of each individual salesperson that works for each partner firm. They may be engaged in support, co-selling, or coordination activities on a large opportunity, working with a partner sales team member, but by and large, their responsibility is to develop the overall partner portfolio capacity, production, and productivity.

This is where Henri was certain he could break down any concern that a hybrid sales channel would turn a direct salesperson into a channel manager. It may turn them into the "general manager" of their own territory, managing all of the resources (direct and partner) that help them exceed their quota. But, that was no different than what he was already working to evolve them to today. Like many other sales organizations, his direct sales force was far more collaborative than those of the past, and he knew that the most successful sales teams are those that can effectively manage and direct as many cross-functional resources as possible in their territory. These teams bring as much perspective as they can to their customers' challenges and in as many ways as possible.

The direct salesperson would need to manage his or her own territory coverage model, focusing on the left third of the figure above—and only the left third—aligning and activating partner sales resources to create coverage and growth. There is little risk that a territory manager in a hybrid sales territory model would become a channel manager by this definition.

What Henri needed to do now was to build out the perfect model and then pilot the concept. He needed to enlist his strongest and brightest sales manager and his "toughest old bird" salesperson with the greatest credibility in the field. If he could engage that ideal team to help him build, model, and create quick win results—even over the objections that would surely come—then he could kindle a concept that would spread like wildfire.

That is what he needed to take to Dominique and Jorge. But first, he had his own phone call to make. Fortunately his sleepless night aligned with daytime in Singapore, where he found Jasmine a ready and willing partner to drive his initial thoughts through to real tactics and execution.

CHAPTER TWO

The Transition: Moving from the Boardroom to the Change Agent

F ast-forward a week from that critical board meeting. Jasmine now finds herself tasked exactly as Henri planned. It's her job to make the principles work in the field and to create the initial model for igniting the organic growth the board demanded. As she prepared to meet John at the Altitude, she concluded that she couldn't lay the responsibility on anyone above her. She had to take it upon herself.

Surely she would need to make sure that John understood the connection between the changes he needed to make and the board-level strategies and resulting tactics that were now in play. In her experience, making this connection would link John directly to something bigger than himself. Failing to do so would allow him to isolate himself from the true need for change. She also knew what was ahead, and it was more than the simple math of dividing the $7 million among channels. Next year, Henri would ask her to get John to grow his $5 million portion to $7 million, and his partner team's portion from $2 million to $3 million. John couldn't handle that kind of growth alone, and she had to lead him to that conclusion.

Jasmine had never prepared more carefully for any customer meeting than she prepared for this meeting with John. She spent hours refining her approach and took counsel and direction from Henri—even doing a mock meeting where Henri played John's role. It was that critical to them both. If they could win over one of the most experienced, influential (in both good and bad ways, depending on his mood), and top-performing members of the direct sales team, their road ahead would be so much smoother. He could be an ally, rather than a critical judge sitting on the sidelines—or worse, a noisy disturbance preventing the alignment of others to the cause.

You've seen the end product of Jasmine's work—the complete cocktail napkin, just before John's agreement and desire to know more.

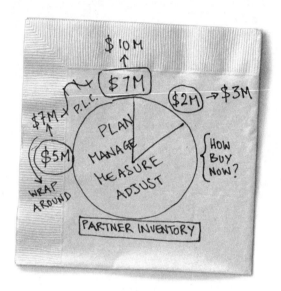

But, beyond $5 million + $2 million = $7 million, what did it all mean? What were the individual elements that Jasmine laid out that became the key execution elements she built from the boardroom objectives? We will fully define all of these elements in the second half of this book when we get into a working model of *The Hybrid Sales Channel*. However, before we dive deeper, let's first look at how the almost illegible end product on the cocktail napkin evolved and listen in on some of the conversation along the way.

1. **Understand how your customers and target customers are buying now.**

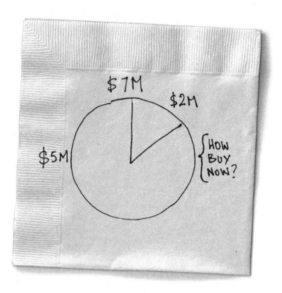

Jasmine was ready to build on that first $7 million circle she had used to get John's attention, but she knew that she would have to engage him by tapping into John's experience working with customers and his unique industry expertise. "John," she said, "let's start with something I think we can both agree on. No matter what you and I talk about here tonight, customers still get to choose. They get to choose from whom they buy, what they buy, how they buy, and when they buy. And if you ask me, their buying process is getting more complex and more unpredictable every day."

Score another point for Jasmine, thought John. And Jasmine was pleased to see that she had John nodding at every word. She was bringing him along like the conductor at a symphony.

"If we're going to have a concrete plan and be able to manage our way to success with you driving only the most high-value targets and solutions, I think it will help if we start by taking a look at how each customer buys now—or at least for starters, every major customer that you think will be part of that $5 million we talked about.

"The customer has to be at the core of our conversation, wouldn't you say, John?" How in the world could a salesperson disagree with that?

And it went on from there. . . .

2. **Inventory all of your current partners who are selling into your customers now—what they sell and to whom they sell.**

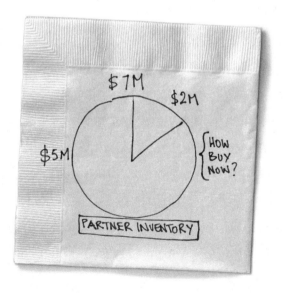

"What percentage of customers in your territory do you estimate currently buy some of our products or services from partners, John?"

John was very quick to get defensive, and his pride, bordering on arrogance, in his ability to personally cover his territory shone through. Despite Jasmine's new ideas, he needed to make sure that she understood he had complete command and control of the space the company had assigned him. "About 15 or 20 percent would be a good estimate, Jasmine. Most of my customers buy directly from me."

Jasmine reached into her case and pulled out a simple spreadsheet that she and Henri had put together in their preparation for this exact part of the discussion. It wasn't elegant. It simply listed every account name that had bought even a dollar's worth of their company's products or services in the last year from a partner, including what was purchased and the total dollar value. Some of the purchases were small, some large. Furthermore, the products represented weren't all what John might have considered their "newest and greatest." The embarrassing truth, however, was that just over 70 percent of John's accounts, by name, were represented on the report. John was floored. At some level or another, 70 percent of his customers were buying from partners?

John sat quietly and stared at the data for a while, but didn't immediately regain his defensive posture. Jasmine let him off the hook a bit, offering up this tidbit to help him process what he was seeing:

"I know, I was as surprised as you when I pulled this together from our channel operations team. Wouldn't it be interesting to discover just who in your accounts these partners are calling on, what business needs they are satisfying, and how strong their relationships are?

"I wonder if your level of customer intelligence were combined with theirs, could you both sell more?"

3. **Map the products you sell in your territory based on where they are in their life cycle.**

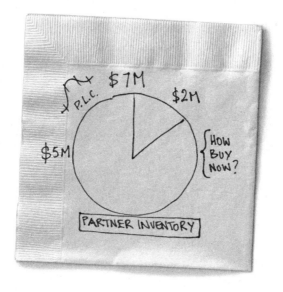

When John and Jasmine took their first look at the spreadsheet, they immediately noted that there was no pattern whatsoever to the product coverage. Some of the partners sold some of the company's absolute newest and most innovative products, while most sold either mid-life or late-in-life products that were becoming more commodity than competition. This observation drove them into a deeper discussion of John's own selling habits and how much time he spent in various parts of his own product portfolio.

"To be honest, Jasmine, I'd like to say that I spend the majority of my time selling our newest stuff. I see that as the place where I can really add value and where my customers expect me and the team to be the expert. But, because I'm inside their hallways wearing our brand so often, I get pulled into all kinds of discussions on almost any product, no matter how simple or mundane. They see me as the 'company guy.' And, I know this happens to our tech support team even more often than it does to me because of the even deeper level of relationship they have with the customer."

John's pride kept coming forward in the conversation, something Jasmine had counted on using as a driving force for change. Jasmine cradled his pride in her words as she carried the conversation on to the next action to be taken.

"Wouldn't it be a worthwhile exercise, considering where we're heading and what we've just uncovered, to do a bit of mapping in your territory, John? Mapping where all of our products and services are in their life cycle, who buys them (and from whom), and how this might help you determine where the $5 million versus the $2 million will come from?

"Can we identify exactly where you drive the highest level of value, get the highest price points, and really leverage your results?"

4. **Identify what products your customers buy that "wraparound" your products to create a total solution to their needs—and from whom they are buying these total solution components.**

Jasmine was a little concerned that she would lose John on the next point. She wasn't yet confident in her own ability to understand the nuances, much less communicate the basics clearly. The devil would be in the details if John started digging in with questions. However, she trusted the coaching she had received from Henri and plunged right into the deep water.

"John, when your customers buy our products or services, what else do they typically buy in order to meet their full needs?"

"I'm not sure what you mean, Jasmine. We've pretty much got every piece of the puzzle our customers need to get the job done."

Step one: Complete.

"Oh, I couldn't agree with you more, John! But, let's think outside of our own box and put ourselves in the customers' shoes for a bit. When our customers have a business need or a problem to solve, is it usually a product need or an actual business result need? When your most senior executive contacts are measured on the results of their work, are they measured on how our products perform or on what business results they create?"

"Well of course you're right . . . I just meant . . ."

Again, Jasmine quickly let him off the hook with a smile and a little laugh. "I know you meant what I meant. Let me show you where I'm going with this." She picked up her pen to draw this next enhancement to the diagram, making it a real mess.

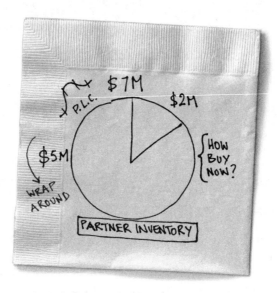

"My point is this. There are other pieces of the puzzle that are not ours—whether products, tools, processes, services, software, or whatever—that combine with our products and services to help our customers achieve the full business outcome they need. Is that a fair statement in your view?"

She kept talking as she continued to draw. "Someone else—perhaps multiple people or firms—are selling our customers those pieces that wraparound our part of the solution. If we clearly understood who all of those players were, what they were selling, how they were selling them, and *to whom* in our accounts they were selling them, do you think that might help us round out our approach to growing our team and getting a bigger share of a bigger pie? Especially if some of those folks are currently aligned with our competitors? Or are currently *our own business partners?*"

5. **Use all of this input to do the hard work: creating a territory plan that leverages John's efforts toward the $5 million of his $7 million quota and aligns the right partners—down to the individual firm and sales rep level—to achieve the other $2 million.**

This last part prompted John to enthusiastically ask, "How do we get started?" There was no more room left on the napkin for the answer to his question, but the fact that John wanted to know the answer left Jasmine with all the room she needed to move forward.

"John, we have a lot of work to do. I'd like us to do the work together. I've got some templates already built that can help us, but they really need your input and practical territory knowledge to polish them up. If we can get this right in your territory, then we can roll it out across the region and maybe across the company. We've got to dial in the way to plan, manage, measure, and adjust as we go along so we can knock growth out of the park for your customers, for you, and for your partners. Together, you and I will have a chance to look like real heroes. What do you think?"

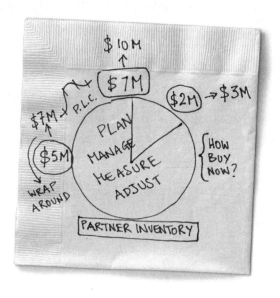

CHAPTER THREE

Cross-Checking the Model Three Ways

To this point we've seen the concepts of *The Hybrid Sales Channel* portrayed primarily from an *internal* company perspective. Before we move on to explaining the "how-to" aspects of the model, there are three perspectives that we need to cross-check against our plan to ensure that it works and is practical:

1. How are partners likely to react to a hybrid coverage model?
2. What impact on customers should be considered at the outset?
3. Where is the optimum point of leverage in designing and managing coverage?

Cross-Check #1: Testing the Approach from a Partner's Perspective

I'm fortunate to have a wonderful neighbor who also happens to be the vice president of enterprise sales at a large value-added reseller (VAR) in the network products and services business and a significant Cisco player here in this region. Prior to moving to the neighborhood, Lane was a sales VP at a telecommunications and cloud services provider, so he has strong experience on both the vendor and partner sides of the channel.

I sat down on Lane's front porch one Saturday to discuss the concepts around a hybrid sales channel. You might imagine that Lane would have some well-founded thoughts and observations on a few of the ideas I tested on him. He's from Texas, so I'd describe him as "politely blunt," wasting little time getting right to the heart of the matter. He took my thoughts in a completely different direction than what I had anticipated.

I expected a discussion of the normal topics from the VAR's perspective: conflict with the vendor's direct team, erosion of margins when the vendor's rep gets involved, and the impact on the end customer (including the age-old argument about "whose" customer it is to begin with). This isn't where our conversation went at all.

He started our discussion with, "You know, Rich, I have the exact same problem."

What I came to understand from our extended conversation was that Lane had the same change management problem that so many of our clients at MHI Global were experiencing—the same problems Dominique and Jorge outlined to Henri in the opening chapters. How do we get the right resources covering the right selling actions on the right opportunities, all without duplicating efforts? It was the same issue, but Lane simply viewed it through a lens that is 180 degrees different in perspective from my own experiences with the issue.

"I have the same problems mapping my resources, aligning my products, looking at market coverage, and turning it into territory plans with my team," said Lane. "The only difference between me and Henri in your example is that I'm getting *my* team to focus on the areas of product and customer where *they can drive the most value*—and then looking to engage members of the vendor's direct sales team to fill holes in my market coverage where they are best suited to sell instead of me.

"The other difference, I suppose, is that I'm reaching out to the vendor to partner into *my* accounts, rather than the reverse."

Funny how that "who owns the customer" comes into almost every conversation about sales. Lane's reference to "my accounts" can't be the first time you've heard a partner use that kind of language and, truth be told, you've probably heard the words come out of your own mouth many times. Partners believe accounts are "theirs" every bit as much as a vendor's direct sales team does. Right or wrong. Good or bad.

Do you remember the scene in *Finding Nemo* where all the seagulls were chasing Nemo's dad and Dory, safely tucked into the beak of the pelican, as they tried to escape? What did the seagulls all say?

"Mine!"

Dozens of seagulls, all saying *"mine"* while chasing the same prey. Do you recall what happened? Sure you do—the pelican flew between a sail and a mast on a sailboat in Sydney harbor, and the seagulls all got caught with their beaks poking out through the sail. Even then, they were all still screaming *"mine"* with their beaks poking out through the sail—as their dinner escaped.

You get the point, just as Lane and I did at the time. No one "owns" a customer. Further into the conversation, it became clear that it wasn't his intent in using the language. Customers buy for their reasons, not yours, and they buy how they want to buy, regardless of how you may want to sell to them. This makes it hard to say you "own" the customer, doesn't it? If not hard, at least less relevant in today's market. Customers are looking for collaboration and perspective, not conflict over ownership. They simply don't have the time for it.

All that said, I was still struck by Lane's perspectives. He runs his own direct sales organization, selling a wide variety of products and services. My surprise wasn't that he has the same challenge. It was in how he looks at it.

As a channel partner, Lane looks at the vendor's direct team as a complementary resource in the marketplace, i.e., one that supports his own direct team. In the same way, Jasmine is working with John to develop a territory plan to collaborate and divest portions of his territory, only to the channel partner team instead of the reverse.

The process is the same. The tenets are the same. The strategy is even the same because the goal is the same— igniting organic growth. You can look at it through either side of the lens, and so long as you focus on aligning the right resource to the right selling action without duplication of effort, everyone wins.

I pressed Lane for an example that would be the equivalent of Jasmine and John. He said the scenario is real and is playing out right now in his organization.

"It's pretty simple, Rich. I've got a former CIO on my sales team who is just outstanding, and as you can imagine, she forges great relationships with CIOs with many of our largest customers. One in particular, a $1.7 billion commercial real estate firm, is one of the finest examples of your principles I can think of.

"We have the highest level executive relationships and are working on the most strategic initiatives of the customer. Most of our business right now, strangely enough, is professional services and not hardware or software. We'll get there, but we're engaged above that level by choice. I'm thrilled with the coverage that we have at that level, but as you can imagine, there is always pressure from our largest vendors to deliver box sales results from this size of an account. While our services will drive huge hardware, software, and networking revenues for us down the road, it's just not where we have our best resources aligned right now."

Lane's got to make every dollar he can and utilize every resource he can. His objectives in that regard are no different than Jasmine and John's. So where does he look? Where does this 180-degree shift in thinking come in?

"I've turned to the vendors and asked them to help cover some of the tactical and functional areas of the account. We have them lining up by technology, application, or departmental functional needs. We've built a much broader team than we could afford to do on our own, and we can still drive revenue and profit that benefit us all. Most importantly, as a team, we're delivering significantly more value to the customer. Some of our partner vendors cover marketing, finance, and logistics leadership, while others cover vertical or horizontal technology specialties.

"We all stay connected on our strategy—the customer's strategy and our account strategy—but we don't have to do all of the same selling activities with the same buying influences across increasingly diverse customers. It's working like a charm so far, and we should be able to leverage it even more once we've really fleshed out our alignment with the most strategic initiatives from the top down. Together, it will be harder to substitute or replace us because we're all aligned on the customer."

There wasn't a table on Lane's front porch, and there wasn't a cocktail napkin. Neither of us needed one. We see things eye-to-eye, whether from opposite points of view or not.

What were the key takeaways from this conversation?

1. Direct sellers don't often give their own business partners credit for the level of independent selling activity they are capable of, the relationships they have, or the complexity of the cross-vendor solutions they are able to sell. Instead, they are often too focused on their own products, still 10 years behind the curve and wondering why a given partner isn't pushing a specific product at the end of a specific quarter.

2. The need for a hybrid sales channel does not begin solely in the vendor's or the partner's boardroom. It can—and should—begin in both. Both links in the chain have the same need to multiply and simplify their efforts, reduce redundancy in sales activity, stay on the same customer strategy page, and create growth for their firm *and for the customer.*

3. Selling is about leveraging resources. Growth is about market coverage. The two have to be brought together. No part of a successful selling engine can create organic growth if there is overlap in selling actions, buying influence coverage, or account coverage.

Cross-Check #2: What Does the Customer Think? Customer at the Core

A common phrase has come into our vernacular in the past decade or so: "voice of the customer."

In business, you can tell when a concept takes off. Job titles with the phrase included start popping up everywhere. Consulting firms are founded with the concept in their name. Departments, initiatives, newsletters, and more contain the new phraseology. It's likely that the language that surrounds "voice of the customer" has become embedded in your own business in marketing, sales, or maybe even across your entire organization.

This terminology comes along with its counterpart: "customer centric."

It's hard to find a CEO or any senior leader in a company who won't declare, often quite loudly, that their company is customer centric. Companies around the world have initiated major strategic, board-level efforts to drive tactics that cause a company to become customer centric. Yet, other than in pure consumer market businesses, there are too few companies where you can find a set of metrics that define what it means to be customer centric and track the organization's progress.

In our story, Jasmine and John didn't begin by discussing the customer at the Altitude Bar. Dominique and Jorge discussed "markets" when talking about creating organic growth. But was the customer's voice present in these conversations? In my discussion with Lane on his porch, we really dug into customer examples of how the partner's view mirrored the vendor's view. Yet, despite the popular appeal of the catchphrases, any change intended to ignite organic growth has to begin with *the customer at the core*.

Many companies, when looking for solutions to the kinds of problems and opportunities sellers face in today's market, look inwardly first. It's their comfort zone. It's the place they believe they can *control*. The board has already spoken loudly, declaring that control-oriented programs that cut costs and attempt to save the way to prosperity are not enough. And yet, the first instinct of most leaders is to repeat the same behavior: consider ourselves, our resources, our practices, our partners, and our organization, and how we deploy them to create growth.

The reason for this illusion of control is simple. *The customer gets to choose.* You can design your routes to market, resource planning, rules of engagement, and all of the elements of your internal and partnering approaches that you like, *but the customer still gets to choose from whom they buy and how they buy.*

This is the first and only reason that all discussions regarding changes in a sales approach intended to ignite growth must begin and end with the customer at the core. It's why Jasmine's first concept in her planning model with John was:

Understand how your customers and target customers are buying now—all the way down to every different type and role of buying influence involved in every level of the sale.

This is a basic element of what it means to have the customer at the core. Customers don't spend time planning how to buy from you. They spend time figuring out how to solve their business problems. We can't start this process by looking from the inside-out. We can only create sustainable organic growth by looking from the outside-in.

The fourth element of Jasmine's planning model also challenged the normal inside-out, non-customer-centric approach:

Identify what products your customers buy that "wraparound" your products to create a total solution to their needs—and from whom they are buying those products and/or their total solutions.

The customer is not solely focused on your products and services. When a customer makes a purchase to solve a business challenge, their need is seldom met by simply buying a single product or stand-alone service. We'll talk more about both of these concepts from Jasmine's planning model and how to activate them in your business. For now, it's important to note that the theme of both is the same: outside-in, customer at the core.

Let's use a very common example to highlight the simplicity of this concept. This one may ring true for many of you based on your personal sales experiences. Here are the symptoms:

You've likely seen this in your own personal forecast, and you've certainly seen these symptoms in forecasts and sales funnels that you've reviewed. There are as many excuses given for the circumstances as there are actual reasons for the reality, but the status is the same: the opportunity is stuck.

What does this have to do with customer at the core? Let's take a look at this simple diagnostic view of what is actually going on:

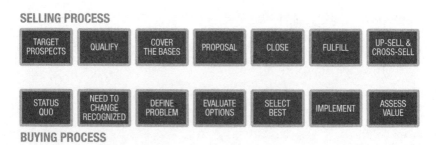

The salesperson completed all of the selling actions and has forecasted the opportunity as ready to close. However, that salesperson forgot to keep the customer at the core. In this case, the salesperson did not stay aligned with the customer's buying process. The customer isn't yet certain of the need to change, but the sales team is certain it is time to close because from an inside-out view, they have done everything their process dictates.

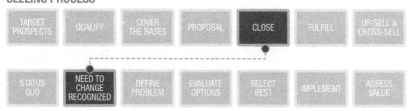

SELLING PROCESS

| TARGET PROSPECTS | QUALIFY | COVER THE BASES | PROPOSAL | CLOSE | FULFILL | UP-SELL & CROSS-SELL |

| STATUS QUO | NEED TO CHANGE RECOGNIZED | DEFINE PROBLEM | EVALUATE OPTIONS | SELECT BEST | IMPLEMENT | ASSESS VALUE |

BUYING PROCESS

Imagine taking this far-too-familiar scenario and plugging it into the complexity of Jasmine's final cocktail napkin. When doing the kind of hybrid territory planning that Jasmine laid out for John, the selling and buying processes are much more complex than this simple depiction. It requires a much deeper understanding than simply knowing where a customer is in a single sales decision. You must also understand:

* How your customers buy
* Who they buy from
* What other products they buy to create a complete solution

Only then can you begin to match up your market coverage and build a hybrid sales channel tailored to how the customer buys. Obtaining results won't be as simple as diagnosing and fixing a few opportunities stuck in the sales funnel. You have to keep the customer at the core.

Before moving on to cross-check #3, let's take a look at the very real risks of implementing the hybrid approach while neglecting to keep customers at the core.

- CUSTOMER RETENTION AND BASE EROSION
- PARTNERS SELL COMPETITIVE SOLUTIONS
- YOUR SALES TEAM SEES THIS "FLAVOR OF THE MONTH" PROGRAM
- NO ADOPTION, CHANGE DOES NOT STICK

The president of one of my largest clients told me this story:

Rich, if I've heard this from a customer once, I've heard it 20 times. The customer looks me in the eye and reminds me that, in the past 10 years, they've had 10 different sales reps assigned to them from my company. Yet in those same 10 years, they've had only one partner firm representing my company to them, and that is who they buy from, regardless of who we might have assigned as our salesperson.

Imagine John were that 10th salesperson and he considered the account "his." (Remember the seagulls.) Jasmine won't get anywhere in extending market coverage for growth until John lets go of his need to control *how the customer actually prefers to buy* and spends his selling time in other places. This is one that Jasmine and John don't have to debate, since they will be setting up their market coverage and identifying where the $2 million is going to come from that John doesn't focus on!

This is the key connection between the boardroom charge and sales coverage execution. When it comes to keeping the customer at the core, it isn't just about slicing the pie differently. *It's about growing the pie.*

If John could bring in his $5 million and partners were capable of bringing in their $2 million from the same base of customers, why bother upsetting the apple cart with unnecessary change? If there is not true growth in the share of customer wallet—true, accretive growth—why bother? The magic of a planned coverage alignment that centers on the *customer,* not the *company,* is that it creates the opportunity for incremental growth—the whole being greater than the sum of the parts.

Cross-Check #3: Can't We Just Solve for This at the Opportunity Level?

No matter how much we try to build systems and processes that keep the customer at the core, there is a never-ending reality with a predictable plot. There will always be some conflict between the direct sales channel and the indirect sales channels, with the end customer caught in the middle.

No matter how much we try to rewrite it, this story always ends the same way. *The customer gets to choose.* The customer gets to choose who they buy from, how they buy, through which channel, and which products and services wraparound yours to complete the total solution to their actual business need. No matter what business model you follow or markets you serve, this is a basic principle that comes into play in every deal!

The inherent conflict we all see between direct and indirect sales models is one of the key drivers for considering a hybrid sales channel. It shows up in competition and conflict over compensation, territory assignment, management control—almost anywhere you might look within the sales function. The source of such recurring conflict shouldn't be surprising when you look at it from the top down.

In most companies, the global head of sales has regional heads of direct sales reporting to them (usually three to six), with only one head of channel sales. By design, the company head count is predominantly in the direct channel since the majority of the head count for indirect channels is out in the partner firms. The vendor gladly gives up some portion of margin to indirect channel firms to be able to scale and expand distribution and sales without adding head count. If you look around the table during any sales leadership staff meeting, it probably looks something like this:

Even though the company may drive a high percentage of its revenue through channel partners, the direct sales head count represented often creates imbalance. The symptoms of the imbalance can be as simple as budget allocation, training focus, or "votes" when it comes to consensus decision making.

On a more complex scale, careers and reputations often get "branded" based on whether someone "comes from direct" or "comes from the channel." In the worst of these career circumstances, sales professionals who are not performing well in direct sales are "given" to the channel organization. The perception of the majority (the direct sales leadership) is that they can be more successful in channel because it is "easier."

What does all of this have to do with Dominique's growth problem and Henri's coverage strategy solution? Everything.

Let's look at a case example I'm very familiar with—a large telecommunications and IT services company working to solve a significant dilemma. This company is an excellent case study and has some key characteristics you may be able to identify with:

- They'd like their indirect channel partners to do more independent selling and less co-selling with the direct sales force (or at a minimum, be less dependent on the direct sales force).
- In order to make progress toward this objective, they've set targets for the percentage of opportunities that are integrated between direct and indirect and, correspondingly, those that are solely channel-sold or direct-sold.
- They've laid out guidelines regarding the characteristics of opportunities that go direct, channel, or co-sold between the two, with a process in place for escalation

and approval of any exceptions. The guidelines are primarily administered at the regional level and driven by the direct sales leadership in consultation with channel sales leadership.

- At the end of the day, they are seeking to grow organically, increase market coverage, and grow market share. Like many other companies, they want to reduce duplication of effort and put the right resource on the right opportunity at the right time. They have problems not dissimilar from Dominque's, just stated differently:

- MARKET COVERAGE IS THE GOAL
- WIDE VARIATION IN EXECUTION
- COMPENSATION GETS IN THE WAY
- PROBLEMS ARE ALWAYS ABOUT A DEAL

This company is not hitting its targets. More exceptions on price, margin, and infrastructure cost are being approved than were planned or expected (or than were built into the financial projections based on the agreed targets and rules). Many of the exceptions are based on compensation impact to the direct sales force. With every exception that gets approved, especially every one that gets approved late in the sales cycle *just to win the deal*, the integrity of their systematic rules of engagement and overall partner plan and coverage model erodes.

They are in the midst of solving these challenges, deciding which best practices and change management strategies they will use to drive their results to a higher level. They are taking Henry Ford's advice: "Don't find fault, find a remedy." Their situation illustrates some common issues that arise when trying to optimize results from multiple sales channels. We asked them to consider three specific questions in their efforts to ignite growth:

Question 1: How Do You Define Market Coverage?

This is, after all, a market coverage discussion. Buyers are going to buy; the question is, from whom and how? When you think about your market coverage model, designing your routes to market, and your alignment between go-to-market strategy and execution, do you think about it at an opportunity level? Do you design your overall coverage strategy with a single sales opportunity as the common unit of measure for aligning resources? Probably not. Yet, this was their design point for making decisions about how to allocate direct and indirect resources. It was also their approach for escalating and resolving exceptions when they occurred. Everything was considered at the opportunity level.

When doing actual market coverage analysis, you consider any number of variables:

- What is my current coverage?
- What white space is uncovered?
- What competitive share do I want to capture?
- Who is currently covering the space I want to capture?
- Where are my products in their life cycles?
- What is the quality of my current resource mix covering the market (skill, enablement, commitment)?
- And the list goes on. . . .

In this coverage discussion, you make decisions from the top down based on revenue and growth targets, taking into consideration average deal size and sales cycle length, and at the end of the day, decide on how to broadly cover certain markets and segments with direct and indirect resources.

Seldom in this kind of a discussion does the concept of a single sales opportunity (or a "deal") come up as the unit of measure for coverage. The closest you may get is at the product level if some products are at a place in their life cycle that dictates either direct coverage (innovative products needing specialized expertise) or indirect (products needing lowest-cost distribution late in life). The leadership imperative for the sales leader when selling a hybrid sales strategy is to go forward sounding bold and positive, something like this:

* We feel strongly that we need to increase our market coverage by eliminating duplication of effort.
* To simplify things, we are going to define a system to evaluate every single sales opportunity and decide which resource, direct or indirect, will sell to that opportunity.
* We'll build a self-correction cycle so that we can make quick course corrections in our rules of engagement to prevent conflict at the partner or the customer level and maximize our customer experience in every sales opportunity.

Question 2: What Is the Scalable Level for Optimizing Multichannel Sales Execution?

By now you may be thinking that defining market coverage at the opportunity level might not be the best answer, but it is the easiest. Partners register opportunities in many indirect channel programs. Direct salespeople manage funnels full of opportunities. Let's just set up our management system at this level—it's easy, it's in our CRM or PRM, and we can report on it and track it.

Unfortunately, easiest is not always best. There are several fatal flaws to consider:

- Opportunities are unpredictable. No matter how good your analytics are, you can't always predict where opportunities come from, how big or complex they will be, and what the perfect coverage will be to capture more of them.

- Resource allocation against opportunities is always suboptimized, for both direct and indirect channels. There is never enough of the right resource at the right time doing the right thing on the right opportunity— especially at the end of the quarter or the end of the year. Product, technical, marketing, implementation, and financial specialist resources are scarce commodities. Trying to plan their availability and utilization, whether for the vendor or the partner firm, at the whimsy of the opportunity funnel is a dangerous gamble.

- Opportunities drive commissions and commissions drive behavior since the core driver of most successful sales professionals is the cash register. To the degree that the opportunity is always available as a lever to be used to create personal income, with or without management discretion, there is opportunity for conflict. Or more. The perception (or reality) of an unfair playing field can be created, and that is very difficult to reverse.

Question 3: If You Do Not Optimize Your Coverage Execution at an Opportunity Level, Which Level Would You Choose?

We can define a sales territory in many ways, e.g., single account, multiple accounts, industry vertical, geography, and other hybrids. Beyond territory definitions and organization, you ideally have a plan for each territory that defines which resources will take which sales and support actions to achieve the desired results.

When thinking about defining rules of engagement and multichannel coverage optimization, our premise is that you might use the sales territory as the basic building block. Just like Jasmine began her discussion with John, you plan your overall coverage strategy by looking at it one territory at a time. You'd start by looking discreetly at each territory and making conscious decisions as to how that territory is covered between channels and resources.

There is no doubt that this is the more difficult path. It takes more detailed planning, which is specific to the territory and the nature of the customers and target markets in that territory. It takes a systematic approach to decide upon a method for creating the right mix of resources to sell into different portions of the territory, even if the territory is a single global or large account. This doesn't necessarily mean taking individual accounts or segments within the territory and deciding that some are direct and some are channel. There may well be good reason for both to co-exist, so long as both are not performing the same selling actions with the same buyers. That will play out and become more obvious as we outline the kinds of tools and analysis available to you to do this kind of work in the next few chapters.

When you have a plan to execute at a territory level, it tends not to fall apart at the opportunity level, so there is less need to build in an escalation mechanism allowing for that. It's a plan that can be designed, implemented, measured, and improved as things change within the market or the territory—*and it is not subject to the whims of what happens with the win or loss of any single opportunity.*

This is where the hard work begins. And it begins now, as we start to create a systematic approach to putting this all in place.

CHAPTER FOUR

Merging Two Methodologies to Ignite Growth

T o create a hybrid sales channel, sales leaders must blend two systematic approaches to selling. For every great idea that started on a cocktail napkin or a boardroom whiteboard, systematic thought and structure must be applied to create predictable results. Wall Street is littered with the meager results of companies with great strategies that were executed poorly.

Our hybrid approach brings together the best thinking and decades of client and industry experience from all five of our sales brand organizations into a simple depiction of how sales systems *work* in real life for our clients around the globe. We call it the MHI Global Sales System™, and it forms the first half of the underpinning of the hybrid.

At a fundamental level, this systematic approach describes how an organization can keep customers at the core while simultaneously managing their business to create world-class sales results. The model is immediately recognizable in the world of direct sales as a representation of what the sales function *does,* providing a structure that allows the organization to identify and improve areas where customer results will have the greatest return on effort. The system is validated by 12 years of research conducted by the MHI Global Research Institute and published in the annual *Sales Best Practices Study.*

In the next chapter, we'll go into detail as to how each of these systematic elements helps build the foundation for *The Hybrid Sales Channel* and help your direct sales team see how their sales skills contribute to the success of the hybrid sales channel.

The core customer-facing elements of this sales system must remain intact in any hybrid sales channel in order for sales results to be truly incremental and to create real organic growth.

In parallel, there are elements of systematic channel management that must be built into the hybrid sales channel in order to make it a true hybrid and not just another "flavor of the month" of a direct sales model. For this, we lean on MHI Global's dedicated channel management and channel sales consultancy to bring elements of the ChannelPRO™ model into the hybrid.

Chapter Six is devoted to the understanding of how the elements of this channel execution model are blended into *The Hybrid Sales Channel* model at the territory level.

For now, let's talk about the fear that is raised by many when they are first introduced to the ChannelPRO model. That is, the terms used and the interconnectivity of the elements may lead some to believe that the goal is to turn direct sales managers into channel managers. Furthermore, they fear that increasing coverage in this fashion will actually decrease the productivity of the direct sales force.

The intent of The Hybrid Sales Channel is to do just the opposite. Using the ChannelPRO model combined with the MHI Global Sales System will allow you to grow the productivity of *both* direct and indirect resources by using a systematic coverage approach *as close to the customer as possible.* Once again, it comes back to keeping the customer at the core.

When we dig into the details, you'll see that it's about application of the hybrid of direct and indirect selling *systems* to create predictable results.

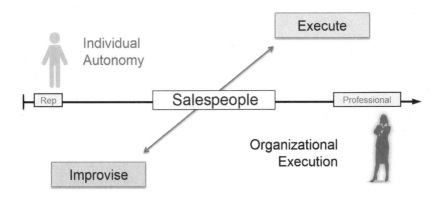

There's not a great deal of mystery to this graphic, but for many, it is a fairly stark look in the mirror. The real question is not about what kind of sales force or sales strategy you *have*, but about what you *desire*. Many organizations desire a high degree of individual autonomy in their sales organizations, and the resulting styles of their management systems and sales culture reflect that desire. Individuals are raised up for their ability to improvise, to be unique. Yet, encouraging this level of individuality and autonomy often leads to less than predictable results.

At the other end of the spectrum is the organization that desires a high degree of organizational execution and values the individuals and teams who execute best and, not coincidentally, deliver the most consistently high levels of results. The Hybrid Sales Channel and MHI Global as an organization are clearly in the camp to right. It isn't that we don't value differences and diversity in a work group or function. Clearly different customers and markets require different styles and approaches. However, these differences need to be *planned*, not random. That is, they must be executed within the context of a systematic approach, and not encouraged within a loose framework that cannot predict outcomes.

As casual as a few notes jotted down on a cocktail napkin or written on a whiteboard may appear, they help lead us to the point where we can dig in deep. Now, we begin the hard work: to prepare, plan, and then execute!

CHAPTER FIVE

Customer at the Core: The MHI Global Sales System™

In this chapter, we're going to introduce the MHI Global Sales System™. However, let's be clear about something from the start. This is not some clever marketing representation of the newest way to talk about the oldest profession. (Yes, sales is indeed the oldest profession, beginning with the first barter of goods or services of any kind between the earliest inhabitants of Earth.)

The MHI Global Sales System is simply a representation of what the sales function *is*. It is what our clients at MHI Global *do*. It is what *we* do. My guess is, in its simplest form, it depicts what your sales organization *does*. Yet, there are some key differences between this model and others you may have seen over the years:

- The customer is at the core. This is simple to say, hard to do.
- It is systematic and interrelated, beginning with the functions that touch the customer directly.
- Management systems are built to be in support of customer-facing activities, not vice versa.

- It is "geared" to be engaged and interactive with all other company functions, processes, and disciplines outside of sales.
- It is not inherently limited to being a direct sales, indirect sales, inside sales, or outside sales model. It exists independent of channel or route to market.
- It does not depict or imply an internally focused approach to the sales function, instead depicting key elements of the functions that enable consistent management of each customer interaction.

Let's look at how the elements of the MHI Global Sales System have been applied so far to create the core elements of *The Hybrid Sales Channel*.

1. **The discussion began with the Customer at the Core.**

Every territory discussion must begin by talking about customers. How can you approach customers differently to create more value? How could a salesperson best use his or her skills to create the greatest value for customers? Where can partners use their abilities to create distinctly different value for the customer?

The idea of keeping the customer at the core may be veiled initially by a discussion about revenues and quotas, but that is just intended to capture the attention of the cash machine—the customer-facing sales force. The deeper you get into any analysis about improving coverage to drive higher growth, the more you will realize that the real discussion needs to be about the customer.

If we go back to the key principles outlined following the board ultimatum, they are absolutely "customer at the core" in their words and meaning: market coverage and alignment of resource to opportunity. This mindset circumvents the normal and common desire to solve every concern and close every gap through organizational change and cost management. Even when making a late-night phone call to their sales leader, our executive champions, Dominique and Jorge, dictated nothing operationally whatsoever. While this is common sense, it is not so common. However, world-class sales organizations put customers before company.

Once the discussion gets into the "how" of operational execution, it becomes even more critical to keep the customer at the core. Changing coverage models can't just be focused on driving productivity for the company and its partners. These initiatives have to create real, measureable value for customers.

Customers have to see that the supplier resources that help them solve their problems or achieve their objectives do several things *better* than any other choice they have. Customers have confidence in these resources because they:

* Know their business.
* Know the full solution needed.
* Bring perspective beyond insightful questions.
* Don't waste their time!

These factors contribute to the customer's perception of value, whether delivered by a partner resource, a direct resource, or a hybrid team.

No wonder Jasmine started (and finished) by focusing on the customer as she laid out her arguments in preparation for her meeting with John. From the beginning, every aspect of the hybrid coverage approach was about keeping the customer at the core:

- How are customers currently buying?
- Which partners are currently selling to your customers?
- What other products do customers buy that surround your products?

Again, easy to say, but hard to do. Your first instincts, or those of your executive team, may not be to look at circumstances through a customer lens. You've got to fight that from the start or you will have lost the battle before it begins.

2. **The initial strategy was framed by the customer core, and it stayed there.**

The board didn't set a strategy, they provided an ultimatum. Organic growth, now! Dominique and Jorge set the strategy, one that kept the customer at the core. They didn't engage a strategy consultant to create three-inch-thick binders that lacked focus on action or operations. Instead, they turned to the leader on their team who had the most frequent interaction with customers and asked him to come up with a tactical plan that could meet the board's immediate expectations.

That brings up an interesting observation. Following the board meeting, Jorge and Dominique did not talk about "what customers say" or "what customers want." They held off, waiting to engage Henri rather than make their own suppositions and assumptions.

All of the discussions leading up to the execution plan had to include and be led by the individuals who have the greatest factual knowledge of what customers want and need. When it comes to separating the best from the rest, the results of *2015 MHI Sales Best Practices Study* bears this out. Data from this research clearly demonstrated that world-class sales organizations leveraged and outperformed the rest of the population in understanding their customers.

	World Class	All Respondents
"We know why our customers buy from us."	89%	70%
"We clearly understand our customers' issues before we propose a solution."	82%	34%

Setting strategies and execution around segment and customer coverage has to be driven by sales, not marketing and not finance. Granted, a great deal of collaboration is required across functions to make this kind of change, but you still need to keep the customer as your compass. You may not have a world-class ability to plan and execute a hybrid sales channel model based on "customer at the core" right now. Some organizations will have further to go than others. Regardless of your starting point, the models and tools in the following chapters are designed to help you close the gap, build a coverage strategy, and execute based on "customer at the core."

You'll recall the conversation we had about why sales leaders aren't invited to speak on analyst's calls. The corollary of this logic is also true. Sales leadership needs to step up and be the voice of the customer inside the company. Real contact with customers will drive real data and rich, fact-based observations that can advise, guide, and self-correct your strategy—provided you keep the customer at the core of your strategy.

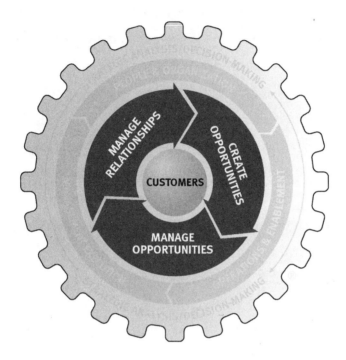

3. **All of the immediate action steps focused on the resources, processes, skills, functions, and people who create value for the customer.**

Simply put, there are three primary selling activities in any business:

- Creating new opportunities
- Managing existing opportunities
- Managing relationships to create new opportunities over the long term

Market coverage and resource alignment have but three goals in mind: increase the quality, quantity, and results from these three selling actions. When Jasmine and John created a plan to manage, measure, and adjust their market coverage and resource alignment, these three selling activities were the levers they pulled to create results.

Why these activities and not others? These are the activities that touch the customer, each day, every day. They are the activities that if executed well (and with the right coverage) will create value for the customer and ignite organic growth. Investments in these three areas create results, something Dominique knew well. After leaving the boardroom, she didn't call her CIO to discuss moving to their third customer relationship management (CRM) system. As important as systems and processes are, they don't *sell*. You can't cover a customer or a market with a computer, software, or process. It's about people and what they do when engaged with customers.

As you'll come to discover, the most critical element in designing your own hybrid sales channel model will be analyzing these three activities across your business. They are the core functions that create value for the customer and are the greatest levers of growth.

By definition, maximizing the effectiveness of every resource at your disposal, direct and indirect, across these three functions means eliminating any duplication. We'll help you find the keys to making the combination of direct and indirect sales forces both *efficient* and *effective* by designing ways to remove duplication of selling actions.

4. **The management system came after the customer-core coverage strategy, not before.**

The death trap for all initiatives of this type is the tendency to start with the outside layer of the Sales System.

It is not our intent to downplay the importance of these key elements to success in the slightest. Instead, we want to highlight where, how, and when they come into play.

As Jasmine's cocktail napkin developed, the territory plan and management system weren't discussed until the very end of the discussion. When she "closed" John on the initial concept, she didn't start out by talking about how they were going to execute and manage it. Nor did she lead with territory change. She started by talking about how customers buy.

If you recall, the management system discussion didn't actually begin until after John said, "You've got yourself a deal! How do we get started?" That's when Jasmine referred to some templates she'd been working on and explained how they could work together to create a territory plan and management system. If she'd shown these first, her plan to convince John would have ended before it started.

There is more to it than just putting the customer-facing elements before the management system elements. While you have to get all of the management system elements right, you can't turn the initiative itself over to the typical owners of the management system for sales: finance, human resources, or sales operations.

To be sure, the Sales System is of critical importance to disciplined, predictable execution. Systems, processes, tools, and people all reinforce the actions that sales professionals make every day to create growth. However, this layer is not an end unto itself and cannot be the leadership engine for change. Change and results happen closest to the customer. They are supported by this layer, not vice versa.

5. **Rebuke the naysayers.**

There's a phrase I hear all the time when talking to very senior sales leaders: "I can't take my people out of the field!" You'll probably hear this as well when you start to build out your change management team and the key stakeholders realize you're asking them to place the change in the hands of those who can make it happen. They may even turn your concept around on you. "We can't take our people away from customers."

Hard to fight that one when we've been preaching "customer at the core" from the beginning, right?

This thinking plays into the trap I mentioned earlier. Instead of allowing the people who know the customer best to shape key change initiatives and drive them to conclusion, sales leaders put such initiatives into the hands of a variety of very critical and able cross-functional groups such as sales operations, sales effectiveness, talent management, human relations, or any combination of the above. These groups may be loosely "led" by a sales leader or tasked with gathering "input" or "buy-in" from sales leaders, but *they themselves do not face the customer every day.*

Dominique and Jorge did the right thing by turning to Henri. In turn, Henri looked to his shining star, Jasmine, to model the way. Jasmine called on the most visible leader who would also be hardest to convert: John. Closest to the customer—customer at the core.

CHAPTER SIX

Infusing the Sales System with ChannelPRO™

I t's going to be a delicate balancing act, to be sure, when creating a hybrid sales channel along with the kind of territory, account, or market "general managers" in the direct sales force who you are going to need to make it work. You can't lose sales momentum in either the direct or partner channel teams. You certainly can't "pull the bus over to the curb" for a complete overhaul. Instead, you must infuse just enough best-practice channel sales DNA into the direct sales force to create the hybrid.

However, this hybridization is not as difficult as it first seems if you have a plan, a system, and a way to measure whether it's working. A systematic channel management model is the last piece of the foundation that needs to be laid before we start building out an actual management approach to the Hybrid Sales Channel. We will lay this final brick by looking at the simplified pieces of the ChannelPRO™ model that can be effectively used by the hybrid sales professional to drive the channel sales resource side of their territory.

The model is shown in Figure 6.1 with definitions for each of the individual components. We will proceed to peel back the layers of this onion and find just those that we need to apply to a hybrid model for direct and indirect sales.

Figure 6.1 *The ChannelPRO Model*

- **Market Mapping**—Choosing which markets and segments you want to sell into. This includes how you plan to reach those customers and the kinds and numbers of partners you need for each segment.

- **Whole Product**—The totality of products, services, attributes, and partnerships that are required to completely meet end-user requirements throughout their buying process—and to actually achieve the desired business results.

- **Partner Selection**—The end-to-end process of setting criteria and managing the selection, evaluation, recruitment, and screening of existing and prospective partners.

- **Channel Enablement**—Working closely with partners through a series of well-defined processes to enable them as quickly as possible to produce revenue for you and for them.

- **Partner Programs**—The policies, incentives, resources, and processes that vendors put in place in order to motivate partners to do the things vendors want them to do and to influence the partner's competitive preference.

- **Sales Productivity**—Using partner planning and review and predictive metrics to drive increased and more profitable results, reducing the impact of role confusion, channel conflict, and unclear rules of engagement.

- **Company Alignment**—Working together and aligned internally with go-to-market objectives; aligned externally with the channel as well.

These definitions may make some of you cringe. Perhaps you're thinking that if we use this model we can't help but violate Henri's principle: *Don't turn sales reps into channel managers!* You saw how Henri began to accept the idea that channel management principles could be applied to his direct sales force to ensure that the right tasks were aligned with the right resources. Keep channel management in the hands of the channel managers, but put channel sales rep engagement into the hands of the direct sales territory managers.

We need to remember a fundamental truth. The direct sales team *doesn't want to* and *shouldn't* manage the channel function. That's the domain expertise of the channel professional.

Here's the critical two-part question:

How can the elements of the ChannelPRO model be tailored to:
A: allow John to drive his $5 million to $7 million next year by focusing on his value and
B: to accumulate a team of partners who can drive their $2 million to $3 million based on their unique value?

Let's take a quick look at each section of the model for clues as to what ideas can be transferred into your own hybrid sales channel management system.

1. Market Mapping: Beginning with Customer at the Core

The first concept Jasmine laid out was clearly an element of market mapping: *Understand how your customers and target customers buy all the way down to every different type and role of buying influence involved in every level of sale. Understand the market, your customers, territory, and industry segments. Understand who buys from whom and why.*

In order to lay out a coverage plan and to become a territory "general manager," John needs to first understand his customers and market and how they are buying.

The second concept of market mapping plays right along: *Inventory all of your current partners that are selling into your customers now, including what they sell and to whom they sell.* This is a subset of the first task that requires honing in on a specific subset of customers to determine their buying behaviors—from existing partners of your company. In order to assess the current coverage of the territory, much less build a plan to ignite organic growth, it's critical to know where your current partners are working and how well they are performing.

As we'll see in the management system itself, this analysis needs to be fairly detailed in order to be effective. At first, general or summarized information may be all that is available. The organization (channel operations, sales operations, marketing, and others) will need to commit to providing the territory team with the best possible data available in order to light the fuse. Beyond that, direct sales professionals will need to do some digging into the existing account, segment, or geographic territory base to pull out some perspectives of their own. After all, no one wants to limit their ability to make decisions that affect income to data provided solely by others!

Wrapping up the front-end work needed to make good "general manager" decisions, Jasmine's third directive comes into play: *Map the products you sell in your territory based on where they are in their life cycle.* This activity should be the easiest for direct sales professionals to relate to and to execute. The descriptions and tools in Chapter Seven will make it even easier.

Simply put, this last step is about aligning the company's products, services, and solutions with the right market resource based on where they sit on an innovation or product life cycle curve. Products that are early in their life and are highly innovative typically require a much higher skill level and depth of expertise to sell. These products are often only or primarily sold directly by the vendor. Alternatively, products that are late in life and nearing a commodity state can only be efficiently moved to market through distribution or other channels that have a lower cost basis. We'll outline this in detail and give you a tool to map sales territories based on your specific products and services in the next chapter.

Have you ever heard it said, *You shouldn't start a race unless you know the distance?* You can't start sprinting if the race is a marathon, and you can't win a sprint at a long-distance pace. Market mapping is about understanding the distance of your race in market and customer terms. When you've done it right, you'll be able to measure the quality of your market mapping by how well the hybrid sales channel coverage you designed eliminates duplicate selling efforts.

2. Whole Product: The "Wraparound"

This step is pretty simple to identify in Jasmine's model, although it won't be quite as obvious as to why she included it in the puzzle. Her fourth directive to John was: *Identify what products your customers buy that "wraparound" your products to create a total solution to their needs—and from whom they are buying these total solution components.*

Let's compare her words to the definition of whole product that we gave earlier:

Whole Product—The totality of products, services, attributes, and partnerships that are required to completely meet end-user requirements throughout their buying process—and to actually achieve the desired business results.

You can see how the concepts match up, even though simplified for Jasmine's sales pitch to John. But, why is this important in identifying a coverage solution in John's territory? Any of a number of reasons might come into play when he is looking to drive growth year after year:

- At a minimum, understanding more about the whole product elements of his customers' solution needs can help him position his own solution's value in light of the value the customer receives overall.
- Knowing the components of solution elements, in terms of value contribution to his customers, will help him understand where his products and services may "sit" in relative importance to his partners when they are selling the whole product.

Are his products the tail or the dog? Which wags which, in terms of customer value?

* Identifying the partners that sell high-value (usually noncompetitive) components of the customers' whole product solution may help John identify the strengths and weaknesses of potential partners for his hybrid plan.

* Partners who are selling ancillary parts of the whole product solution to the customer may or may not be current partners of John's company. Those who are not could be potential recruitment candidates for the channel managers. Once on board, their existing relationships and value in the customer or market base will also be available to John for his hybrid plan.

This part of the planning can be simplified and streamlined. It may be relatively easy for product marketing, channel marketing, and other internal sources to provide potential partner profiles to John and his peers. But, the potential to leverage the whole product as a source of organic growth can't be overlooked as a part of the total plan. The whole product territory analysis tool in Chapter Seven will help you make use of this concept regardless of your business, sales model, or industry.

3. Partner Selection: The Keys to the Kingdom

This step is where "the rubber meets the road" at the territory level: With whom am I going to align to make the $2 million that I am not going to focus on myself? Well-executed partner selection at the territory level demonstrates your ability to collaborate in your own hybrid sales channel and prevents much of the seagull behavior before it can start.

This is also the place to demonstrate that a hybrid channel will not turn John into a channel manager—Henri's worst fear. We're not talking about partner selection in terms of targeting or selecting new partner *firms*. We're looking at the partner salesperson level. This is so important, I want to repeat it. John's hybrid sales channel is made up of individual partner sales professionals, *not partner sales organizations.*

Who are the individuals who can join in the pursuit of the $2 million goal? Surely there will be gaps and places where there are not sufficient firms or resources to cover the territory, but those requirements can be fed back to the channel management team. John needs to handpick his team from the resources currently available to him.

If John has done his homework and has confidence in the process and criteria he's used to select his partner teammates, then he can be off to the races, knowing he has only to concentrate on his own value contribution. If he has not chosen wisely, he'll be constantly looking over his shoulder, second-guessing himself and his chosen partners. Or worse, he'll resort to covering the whole $7 million himself and not gain the market coverage leverage he'll need in future years.

By combining the data from market mapping and the perspectives from his whole product analysis at a channel partner sales professional level, John will gain clear insights into which partner sales professionals he needs to enlist for his team and why. The better the information, the better he'll feel about his selections.

Your own channel management team should be able to provide some of the broader selection and evaluation criteria they use as basic guidance. Their partner scorecard or equivalent data about the characteristics of each firm form a good starting point. In addition, there will be cases where a great partner firm championed by a channel manager doesn't have the right skill set or coverage to match the requirements in an individual territory. At the end of the day, you need to focus on partner sales professionals who are right for the territory, not make decisions based on a partner's popularity within channel management. It's not like picking a team on the playground. This is serious.

4. **Channel Enablement: Is This Really My Job?**

In a classical channel management world, channel enablement is one of the functions that contributes the most to the success of the partner and the partnership.

It is also one of the most critical job functions of the channel manager and his or her support team.

In a hybrid sales channel, the role of channel enablement must never become the job of the direct sales professional. Direct sales professionals are skilled at managing opportunities, one-on-one. Channel enablement includes a number of tasks that sap productivity if attempted at the individual partner sales professional level:

- Product technical and sales training
- Competitive market knowledge and the vendor's value differentiation
- Marketing and tool training in the vendor's PRM and related systems
- Administrative training in all of the ordering, billing, credit and returns, licensing, and myriad other processes and procedures that the vendor requires a partner to follow
- Knowledge of the vendor's partner program

You can see how Henri's greatest fear might be realized if every one of the direct sales professionals spent time on these sorts of tasks. That's what can happen when an organization doesn't make the effort to integrate the ChannelPRO model with the MHI Global Sales System™.

But let's not drop the subject too quickly. John's personal success absolutely depends on his ability to enable the individual partners he brings into his hybrid coverage model. It's just a different kind of enablement.

To identify the keys to success, think about some of the change management initiatives or new process implementations in your own organization. You can focus either on the ones that have gone well or on those that have gone not so well in your own organization. The questions are the same:

* Is there a connection of the change to an overall strategy?
* Is there a connection of the individual to his or her impact on the strategy and its goals?
* Is there an attempt to show individuals how they can make a difference and how that will impact them personally, professionally, and (especially in sales) financially?
* Is there a structured, ongoing communication process that extends beyond the initial presentations, slide decks, and high-level emails?
* Are there metrics that tie individual performance to overall performance of the change?

For the direct sales professional in a hybrid model, these elements become the framework for creating the kind of enablement efforts that will ensure success. As John moves from seagull behavior to open and collaborative selling in his territory, he will need to make some changes. His role in sales enablement will be to bring a team of territory partners along on a new journey. His role will look and feel more like that of a sales manager at times, without the sales manager's ability to "tell others what to do." He'll have to adopt Jasmine's ability to coach and influence in order to help others change, and to make change stick and create results.

The channel manager for any of the partner firms John ends up selecting can take care of the broader elements of enablement, including educating on the strategy, how it connects to success for both firms, and how it is going to be executed, measured, and rewarded. With each individual partner sales professional that is on his team, John's role is much more hands-on. He should focus his time on activities like:

* Creating clear definitions and mutual agreement on the roles and responsibilities inside the territory, especially within any individual account.

- Building knowledge-sharing processes to disseminate information about individuals inside an account, including roles, degree of influence, attitude toward the vendor or partner, relevant background, etc. Knowledge sharing must include changes in any of these elements that materially affect the potential for success of the partnership.

- Communicating trends or opportunities that exist or appear in a customer's business or marketplace that may create new selling opportunities.

- Immediate sharing of any risk exposures such as:

  1. Competitive threats or changes in position by key competitors
  2. Failures in execution of any kind
  3. Organizational changes, announced or unannounced
  4. Arrival of new key buying influences from outside the organization

- Committing to a regular cadence of communication, metrics reviews, and actions to be taken.

These are the kinds of sales enablement responsibilities that will make John successful in the end if they are done correctly from the beginning. They can be the early roadmap for the success of the hybrid sales channel in his territory.

5. Partner Programs: Taking Advantage

Every vendor has a documented partner program that explains the "rules of the road." These programs typically define the benefits that will be accrued by the partner in exchange for their investment of resources, and they define how the partner will be rewarded for results. They also outline the resources and investments that the vendor is willing to put in place to support and help the partner firm grow their business based on the investments and results the partner achieves. The programs are often updated annually and are treated as a component of the vendor's overall strategy for channel sales and a statement of the vendor's partnering philosophy.

As you can imagine, the programs are not the place for a hybrid territory sales professional to be spending his or her time! There are plenty of "partner program lawyers" on both the channel partner and vendor side of the table, interpreting the details and discussing how the programs can help promote consistent execution and predictable results.

When it comes to the partner program, John has but one mission. Take advantage of the elements of the program that will make his territory partners most successful and translate these elements into actions that create sales. More sales. Better sales.

Some simple examples will help illustrate the point:

• How can the market development funds (MDF) that are often available through the partner program be leveraged at the territory level within John's key partners?

• What periodic incentives (fast start, quarterly, first half, etc.) in the program align with key opportunities where John's partners are going to be taking the lead? How can these be identified to help drive the right "early win" partner behavior?

- What specific product incentives line up with the analysis of partners that John did when looking at where they are in covering products at different places in the life cycle? How can these incentives help John aim the right resource at the right product segment?

By using the partner program to help focus and drive the desired behaviors on the part of his channel partners, John can increase his odds of success while staying focused on his own segments of his territory. If ignored as an element of the approach or done poorly and without structured thought, these programs are an opportunity lost.

6. Sales Productivity: Measuring Without Managing

Let's remind ourselves of the definition of "sales productivity" in the context of the ChannelPRO model and
how it relates to creating a hybrid sales channel.

*Sales Productivity—Using partner planning and review
and predictive metrics to drive increased and more
profitable results, reducing the impact of role confusion, channel conflict, and unclear rules of engagement.*

Whew! If that doesn't sound like channel management, what does? Once again, John should be able to
count on his channel manager partners and the company's processes and systems to provide the core of what
is needed to drive success in this arena. However, it's
not the role of the channel organization to scale their
efforts down to the level of the specific partner sales
professionals in John's hybrid team.

To be effective and efficient, John needs to create
plans, conduct reviews, and define metrics that are
practical, actionable, and *mutually agreed upon.* Let's
look at these in reverse order:

- **Mutually Agreed Upon**—The metrics, planning,
  and review processes in a hybrid model can't be
  imposed on channel partners. Nor can they be
  the vendor's standard template, born out of John's

historically seagull-like behavior, or those insisted upon by the partner firm and its overall standards. While any and all of these can form a basis for what ends up being the final management system, it is absolutely critical that both parties mutually agree upon what will be used: what, why, when, and how. Anything less invites resistance or apathy.

- **Actionable**—The metrics need to be equally balanced between *actions* and *results*. That is, you need to create a balance of leading metrics and trailing metrics. This is even more critical in the early stages of an individual territory hybrid when success may not come as quickly as desired. Too much focus on results can easily leave both sides dispirited. In order to get quick wins on results, you must first measure and celebrate quick wins on actions and activities.

- **Practical**—You can't manage what you can't measure. The system of management and measurement in a hybrid sales channel must be drawn from things that can be measured *today* by both parties, not a wish-list of things we would like to measure but don't have the systems or the data to do so. John and his hybrid partners will know what is practical for them to measure between themselves to create results. They should leave the rest to parties above and beside them in the organization that can afford to take a less pragmatic view of the world. Practical metrics, planning, and systems keep the customer at the core.

But, what of the subtitle of this section: *measuring without managing*? Isn't all measurement aimed at feeding a management system? In the case of a hybrid sales channel, the message is more specific and in line with what we've already described: instead of being concerned about turning direct sales professionals into channel managers, the management and measurement system has to support them in being ready to be territory general managers.

If we believe in the premise that partners do things for their own reasons and not for the vendor's reasons, then it follows that partners do not want to be managed as if they are the vendor's direct sales force. While successful channel managers have learned this by running headlong into this reality many, many times, John has yet to experience it. *Seagull behavior can easily lead to a notion that his hybrid partners should be managed as if they work for him and not with him.*

The management system itself—practical, action-able, and mutually agreed upon—needs to reflect this reality. It is a partnership, not a one-way street.

7. **Company Alignment: All on the Same Page, Inside and Out**

There's a strong argument to be made for beginning an initiative with company alignment. After all, isn't that what the board, Dominique, and Jorge set out to do? Can you really get anywhere without having your company aligned from top to bottom on a change as significant as the hybrid sales channel?

Beyond the sense that market mapping keeps the customer at the core (and is therefore our initial compass), there is a more basic reason for ending with company alignment rather than beginning with it. The nuance is at the end of the definition of company alignment.

Company Alignment—The need to work together, to be aligned internally with go-to-market objectives, and to be aligned with the channel as well.

The addition of the words "aligned with the channel as well" in the definition makes all the difference. Let's talk about that a bit.

You probably won't be surprised to hear the kinds of opening questions I often get from senior-level sales leaders seeking to improve their channel performance. These may not be in the exact order of frequency that I hear them, but pretty close, top to bottom:

- The distribution of our revenue across our partners is a mess. Can you help us with our partner selection criteria so we can find the right partners (a.k.a. better partners)?
- Our partner program isn't driving the results we're looking for. Can you help us redefine our incentive tiers and components and share some industry best practices that will drive better and more consistent results?

- We're experiencing a tremendous amount of channel conflict between partners and between our direct force and our partners. Can you help us look at our rules of engagement and see where there might be opportunities to reduce conflict and get back to normal healthy competition?

Perhaps you've been one of the clients on the other end of my phone. Maybe you've even turned to other thought leaders, inside or outside of your company, for a second opinion. What sorts of answers have you gotten?

To be sure, these are valid questions, and there are valid best-practice answers to these and many other channel sales challenges, *but these questions portray symptoms, not the core of the issue.*

Prior to digging into these or any number of detailed issues, I always investigate one thing. What is the degree of alignment that exists today? Does this alignment exist:

- Above sales leadership, on the go-to-market strategy?
- At the top of sales leadership, on the balance of routes to market to meet customers' buying preferences?

- Across sales leadership, direct and indirect, as to how to move from strategy to tactics to accomplish critical jointly agreed-upon objectives?
- Between the company and its partners, in relation to the end-customer market as well as mutual objectives of the company and the partner firms in serving those markets?
- And on goes the list. . . .

This is where *"and aligned with the channel as well"* comes into play as the reason to finish, not begin, with company alignment. It isn't about beginning with or ending with this element of the model. It's about sustaining, maintaining, and measuring alignment *throughout* the journey. Not only through "customer at the core," but also through engaged partners and tightly interwoven, cross-functional internal teams.

While I often begin a consulting engagement or a senior leadership conversation with alignment conversations, the leaders never, ever succeed unless they are also steeped in the detailed elements represented by the modules of ChannelPRO. The quick answers to the easy questions never come without digging deep into the details, and the details are always interconnected just as the elements of ChannelPRO are.

It is not only important to be aligned internally, but also tightly aligned with your partners. You'll build that as you design and create your hybrid sales channel, but you probably won't start there. First, you need to put some hard work into the other elements. Then you'll be ready to be aligned on a completely systematic approach to the details that keep the customer at the core.

CHAPTER SEVEN

Preparing for Territory-Level Execution of The Hybrid Sales Channel

J asmine had led John to the point where they could prepare to execute with these words:

John, we have a lot of work to do. I'd like us to do the work, together. I've got some templates already built that can help us, but they really need your input and practical territory knowledge to polish them up. . . .

That's where we will resume our discussion. Make no mistake. This is where the hard work begins. We must now turn all of the concepts and frameworks into actions that will actually ignite growth. In this chapter, we will take it layer by layer. From there, you should be able to build your own workable approach by adding practical territory knowledge before you add your final polish and present the plan to your organization.

A Key Concept Before We Begin: The Red Flag

My good friend Bob Miller, founder of Miller Heiman along with his partner Steve Heiman, coined the term "red flag" back in 1985 in their book *Strategic Selling.* Over the years, it would be hard to find a sales professional or sales executive who doesn't regularly use the term in their daily language of selling. In addition, I'm quite sure it's crossed over into many cross-functional areas of business outside of sales. I'm also sure, because he's chided me many times, that Bob was very precise in how the term "red flag" was to be used when talking about a sales scenario. That precision may have been lost over time. We're going to use the concept here, so let's get it right!

The term was originally chosen because it was almost universally recognized as a signal for "warning" or "danger." In that sense, a red flag is not a *bad* thing. It is a *good* thing! It alerts you to a condition that, if not attended to, can threaten your chances of success in a selling situation. Red flags call your attention to potential issues in time to do something about them.

Bob and Steve identified five areas of sales strategy that should automatically be considered red flags. As we look at Jasmine's templates throughout this section of *The Hybrid Sales Channel,* you'll see a number of red flags in various sections of the analysis. Many of them are representative of one of these automatic red flag scenarios:

1. **Missing Information**—What information is incomplete or unavailable at present that, if not obtained, could cause you to create a faulty solution design or selling strategy?

2. **Uncertainty About Information**—What information do you lack confidence in, perhaps because of its source, quality, or completeness? How would your approach be at risk if the information you have is wrong?

3. **Uncontacted Buying Influences**—Are there individuals who you have not contacted or taken into consideration when mapping your coverage of the right resource to the right selling action and customer contacts? What risk is created if you do not understand these gaps and have a plan to close them?

4. **Buying Influences New to the Job**—Are there new players involved in key buying influence areas in accounts where you are building a hybrid team? How does what you know (or do not know) about them influence your coverage model decisions?

5. **Reorganization**—Are there any recent or pending reorganizations in your territory or within a customer that challenge your initial thinking about how to align resources and create customer-facing partnerships?

Any of these factors can cause your analysis—and therefore the design and execution of your coverage strategy—to be at risk of being faulty at best. When in doubt, identify the risk with the placement of a red flag, and work to remove the red flag by getting more information or better information before finalizing the input of that factor into your decision making.

With that under our belt, let's move on to the key tenets that Jasmine laid out for John.

Understand how your customers and target customers are buying now—all the way down to every different type and role of buying influence involved in every level of sale.

This first step in the territory analysis takes us back to the basic principle: Customer at the Core. It's easy to *say* that we will begin by looking at how our prospects and customers are buying now, but it's much harder to *do*. Why is it so hard?

- Buyers' behaviors, especially the behaviors of individual buyers, are far too great a mystery to too many sales professionals. We base our careers on our ability to influence buying behaviors, yet most often find that we have too few facts to sell with confidence. Fortunately, to do the work required in this step of analysis, we only have to focus on *what* buyers are doing and not the more difficult *why*.

- Just as there is no prototypical sales professional, there is no prototypical buyer or buying influence. Each one is unique. Therefore, the work to understand them is difficult. There's an old adage that could not be truer: *Beware of someone who generalizes about something of which they do not understand the details.* When it comes to buyers, we have to get into the weeds.

- When we're looking to transition a sales territory into a hybrid approach, there isn't a single size or model that fits all. Different kinds of territories require different kinds of customer analysis:

  1. **Single, Large, or Global Account Territories**

     These territories are more complex organizationally, yet have the benefit of both scale and institutionally available information (both public and private). An analysis of how the customer buys can be performed by business unit, organizational function, reporting structure, or any number of methods.

  2. **Industry-Segment or Vertical Territory**

     In territory segments by industry or vertical, more generalizations can be made because the businesses within the segment share similar characteristics. However, an analysis should still be performed because their organizational, functional, or business unit challenges will be unique, especially when there is a range of company sizes.

  3. **Geographic Territory**

     Perhaps the most complex of all the models, this type of territory can be defined by anything from postal codes to states or provinces to whole countries. With few inherent similarities between customers, the geographic territory requires perhaps the highest level of generalization about how customers currently buy. The analysis can be made more specific by breaking down the territory into subgeographic segments or using some elements of the other two territory types for analysis purposes (e.g., major accounts or key industries within the geography).

Let's start with a tool concept that can be applied to each territory type. It's simple, yet flexible enough that you can blend and morph the tools to fit your particular circumstance. We'll walk through the territory types one by one, but by the time we take a look at the first, the others will be pretty self-explanatory.

The Major Account Territory

This is the one you have to get right. These are your largest accounts, the place where you have both the highest risk and the highest opportunity for reward. At the same time, these accounts are also ones where you can be certain that partners of yours (and partners of your competition) are already calling, selling, and maintaining relationships. The questions are: *How is the customer currently behaving, and how can I use that knowledge to my advantage?*

This tool may look too simplistic for such an important territory type, but its elegance is in how you apply and use it. Let's take a look at what lies on and behind the blackboard:

SINGLE ACCT	YOU	COMPET	PARTNERS	?
VP MKTG			X	
CIO	X	🏴		
CFO		X		
VP MFG				🏴

Hopefully this looks as simple as we predicted it would be. In this example, we're looking at a single account territory by executive title, but you could change the left column to reflect titles within business units, functions across business units, or almost any criterion relevant to your business. The analysis is just as easy to perform. Who does the specific buying influence predominantly buy from *now*, when it comes to *purchases designed to achieve the results your products and services can offer?*

The simplicity is the key to actually getting value out of the analysis. You gather information from a variety of internal and external sources, find out more, and use it to inform your approach going forward. If you make the analysis too intensive, you'll get less buy-in internally and externally—and poorer quality results.

As you begin this phase of hybrid territory design, there are some basic precepts that will apply across every territory type and partner analysis. You're talking about your relationships—those you have, those your partners have, and those you wish you had. Some critical elements apply to keeping this particular analysis real:

- **Keep It Simple**—Don't overcomplicate the analysis or begin with too broad a list of buying influences. You can develop more breadth and depth over time, but starting with too long a list may create paralysis by analysis and lead to inaction instead of action. Focus on the *key* buying influences that you personally are getting business from, and those that you are not. Don't just focus on your friends, the easy ground, or the places where business has come from in the past. Have an eye to the future, to changing business models and directions, and consider what your coverage has been *as well as what it needs to be.*
- **Check Your Ego at the Door**—Be honest with yourself about the quality of relationships that you have, as

well as the access and degree of influence in existing and future buying influence roles, positions, and titles. Have your relationships led to actual business, or is the business going to someone else? If you believe there are partner sales professionals who may be positioned or better capable of being positioned in the future to influence certain roles, identify them! If you know of competitive incumbents in parts of the business, and whether you have current relationships in the same areas where those buying influences live, make sure to identify them, too. Don't let your ego get in the way, thinking that only *you* are capable of selling to these roles. This is no time for seagull behavior.

- **Remember the Concept of the Red Flag**—The presence of a red flag is good, not bad! It highlights what you don't know or what you need to get better information on. At first, there are going to be many places where you don't know for certain to whom a given buying influence is sending their business. You may know that there are certain partners involved in your account, but you're not sure exactly where their relationships are. You may not be certain whether a competitor has stronger coverage or a lasting relationship with a buying influence that is driving business—or if it's just "golf course coverage." All of these things are red flags that represent risk to your strategy, and it is worth the effort to gather more information so you can remove them.

The goal here is to be good, not great. Get something on paper that represents the first part of the analysis so that you can move on to the second. This will give you a baseline knowledge to track your progress against going forward. After all, the journey has just begun.

Industry-Segmented Territory

There are two variations of the industry-segmented territory—a territory that is made up of a single industry vertical or a territory where accounts or prospects are segmented by industry rather than by account or geography. The former is fairly simple. Instead of a single large account, you have a number of accounts in the same industry that have many similar characteristics (e.g., marketplace, business model, go-to-market strategy, buying models, etc.).

There is no reason you couldn't use the major account territory model we just discussed and apply it to a single industry vertical. However, there are a few differences you may want to consider. Unless the number of accounts is small, it would be difficult to get down to the individual buying influence in your first coverage analysis. Therefore the first column is less likely to be names or titles and more likely to be accounts or divisions (business units or other segments) of accounts. In addition, industry symmetry may make it easier to identify the partners or competitors winning business in your accounts as there will be fewer likely suspects.

Your industry-vertical territory analysis is likely to be a blend of the major account analysis, the suggestions we just covered, as well as ideas gathered from others. The key is to get something down on paper and start to play with it. Improve it. Share it. Get feedback.

It is more challenging to do an analysis for a multi-industry territory where you segment the territory with industry-based products and solutions to match. Perhaps you have just a few industries, perhaps several. No matter the scenario, this kind of segmentation requires the same analysis of how customers are currently buying, but one that is tailored to the unique territory characteristics.

INDUSTRY	YOU	COMPET	PARTNERS	?
HEALTH CARE	X	X		
FIN SERVICES		🏳	X	
MFG	X	X		
DISTRIBUTION		X	X	

The same rules apply in this analysis (keep it simple, check your ego, use red flags) as in the major account territory analysis. It many ways, you may find the analysis easier in an industry-oriented territory than in a territory with a single large account. Because of their industry specialization, competitors and partners can be much easier to identify and align to the segments where they are winning business.

The approach of the analysis remains the same as you begin to dissect your territory to decide where to focus your coverage. Get facts, not opinions or judgments. If you understand where others are winning business, you will have a better chance of deciding whether you can or should compete for that business. And if it makes sense to do so, what kind of sales coverage is best based on how the customer is buying now.

Geographic Territory

This is the kind of territory I had when I started my sales career. At first, I supported the entire state of North Dakota and the northern portion of Minnesota. Later, I graduated to just covering the southern third of Minnesota. While the weather was marginally warmer, and the accents sounded slightly less like those in the movie *Fargo,* the characteristics of my territory remained the same regardless of how far south I went.

- I was responsible for every account within the geography.
- Every industry possible was represented within the territory: manufacturing, financial services (although back then we simply called it banking and insurance), utilities, local and state government, distribution, health care, etc. I had to be truly a "jack of all trades, and a master of none" when it came to my customers' businesses.
- In my case, the geography was vast. Some of my colleagues covered geographies such as New York City or Singapore where their challenge was density rather than distance.

Again, we have the same whiteboard analysis, just reconfigured for this type of territory design. Often, the more senior, experienced sales team members think this type of territory is the simplest, easiest, and most "fun" sort of selling. Indeed, the impression of managers with large account or vertical territories is that the geographic territory is full of places where a sales professional can hide. However, when building a coverage plan for a hybrid sales channel, this type of territory takes the most work and can be the hardest.

Calling this type of territory "geographic" leads to the first part of the analysis for many. Many of these territories include one or more countries, provinces, states, or other large geographic regions. In most cases, it makes sense to begin your assessment of how customers are buying based on geographic subsegment.

GEOGRAPHY	YOU	COMPET	PARTNERS	?
CITY 1	X		X	
CITY 2			X	
STATE 1		X		⚑
STATE 2	X		⚑	

Your company will be more successful in some geographies than others for any number of reasons: industry concentration, distribution capability, distance from customer service, technical support, and so on. While your competitors have the same challenges, they will not have the same success profile that you do. Do an honest assessment of both your profile and theirs so you can begin with a solid baseline of facts.

The same is true of partners—perhaps even more so. Being entrepreneurial in nature, many business partner firms have geographic specialization models or capabilities. Where are those that align with your company's value propositions located? Where are they winning business already? Let's not worry yet about *what* customers are buying from partners, much less *why*. For now, especially in a geographic territory, we need to begin by understanding *where* partners are already winning business.

Now, here's the reason this kind of territory is so complex and difficult to analyze for market coverage. The other two models also apply. To the degree that important industries or key/large accounts exist within the territory, you'll want to do some level of analysis of who is winning business for each segment. You may not have the time, energy, or detailed knowledge to perform a complete analysis, but one simple measure can tell you how much energy to put into this. *How much of your quota is contributed by a handful of accounts or concentrated in a few industries?* The more concentration you have, the more work you'll want to do because it will give you leverage with your hybrid sales channel coverage model.

At this point, you are probably asking, "Where can I get the information I am going to need?" You may be surprised to find that you have 80 percent of the information you need to complete this level of coverage analysis all by yourself. Here are a few resource ideas that can help you fill in the knowledge gaps and eliminate more red flags.

- **Competitive Analysis from Your Marketing Department**—This is a good time to cash in on favors to get the most granular competitive data you can from your internal marketing team. If you are driving this kind of a coverage program from a sales leadership position, do your sales team a big favor and get as much data as possible prior to rollout so they can be productive faster and not have to waste time searching for it.

- **Partner Sales Data from Your Channel Marketing Department**—Depending on the type and quality of information your partners and customers share with your company, your channel team may be able to report with some level of granularity which products have been purchased in your territory. Reach out to them and see what you can get.

- **LinkedIn and Other Social Connections**—If you want to know where your competitors are imbedded, look at the social networks of your key buying influences. How many of your first-level customer contacts have more first-level contacts within competitors than they do within your company?

- **Reference Logos on A Competitive Website or Other Published Sources**—Companies love to show the logos or names of their customers on their websites or in presentations they give to analysts or industry groups. Who is represented in your competitor's public presence, and what might it say about their foothold in your territory?

Inventory all of your current partners that are selling into your customers now, including what they sell and to whom they sell.

At this point John may be second-guessing his statement, "You've got yourself a deal! How do we get started?" Jasmine didn't promise him the work would be easy, only that she was going to ask him to focus on $5 million of his $7 million quota. You'll remember that she said something about having a lot of work to do.

Let's leave behind the multiple ways of looking at customers and territories. Once you understand how your customers are buying now, you can adjust the second step to be exactly what you need to fit your circumstances. After all, templates drawn on whiteboards are written with erasable ink!

This next step gets a little more specific than the first. Rather than just asking who customers are buying from, you'll need to uncover specifically which partners are already selling into your accounts.

The reason is simple, but the math is profound. If the partner is already selling into some portion of an account, they already have relationships and are satisfying needs. Since we know it costs much more time and money to create new sales relationships than to leverage existing ones, it makes sense to know which specific partners are already active inside your territory.

They may not be selling to the same buying influences you are. They may not be selling your leading-edge products or services. They may not even be selling the same applications of the products and services that you are. But they're already there, so let's understand specifically where they are.

There are several ways you could look at this analysis, such as finding out which partners are present within which customers and, if your channel or product marketing team can get you the detail, which partners are selling which products into a given customer. Based on your own relationships with buying influences at departmental or functional levels, you may be able to take the analysis even deeper and look at which roles your partners are selling to.

The work is worth doing. After all, you may find out that the customer is tolerating the most recently assigned sales professional from your company but that they have been buying from a favored partner for years. Or at least the customer may see it that way.

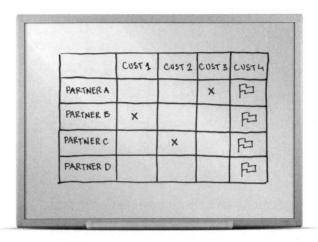

Partner Coverage Across Multiple Customers

	CUST 1	CUST 2	CUST 3	CUST 4
PARTNER A			x	⚑
PARTNER B	x			⚑
PARTNER C		x		⚑
PARTNER D				⚑

PARTNER A	PROD 1	PROD 2	PROD 3	PROD 4
CUST 1		x	x	
CUST 2	x			⚑
CUST 3		x		
CUST 4				

Single Partner Coverage by Product Across
Multiple Customers

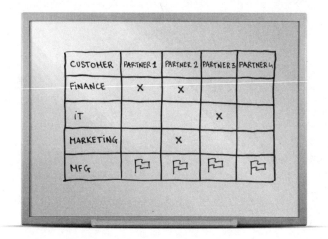

Multiple Partner Coverage Analysis by
Functional Role Inside a Single Customer

Map the products you sell in your territory based on
where they are in their life cycle.

Let's take a brief break from whiteboards and cover an important concept: the relationship between product life cycle, market coverage, and customer buying expectations and habits. It starts with a relatively simple curve, drawn for the sake of simplicity as a "bell curve" that is familiar in shape and concept. You may have seen it in the upper left-hand corner of Jasmine's cocktail napkin and asked yourself, "What does that bell curve have to do with this coverage analysis?"

Here is a slightly more elegant version of Jasmine's hand-drawn version.

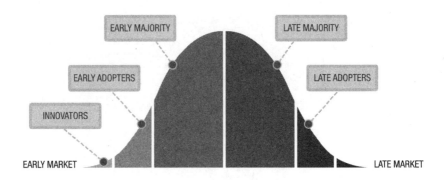

The curve, with its labels, is self-explanatory. It describes the life cycle of a product and its relationship to the types of customers who buy the product during its useful life in the market. So, what does this have to do with a territory market coverage strategy and building a hybrid sales channel?

Let's answer this question from the outside in, using our Customer at the Core concept. Before we focus on your products and where you think they may be on this curve, let's first look at the customer categories that span the life cycle of any given product. From left to right we have:

- **Innovators**—These are people who just have to have the latest thing. They are the first people on your block to have the newest technology, even before there is any content available that can take advantage of the advanced features. There may not be many of these people, but winning them over can be really important because they reassure the other players in the marketplace that the product does in fact work.

* **Early Adopters**—Like innovators, this group buys into new product concepts very early in their life cycles. Unlike innovators, these people don't want the product or service just because it is new. They are good at conceptualizing how this new product or service might give them business benefits, sometimes even before the vendor's marketing department manages to figure it out. These people are looking for *competitive advantage.* They are key to opening up markets because they don't rely on well-established references when making buying decisions.

* **Early Majority**—These customers share some of the early adopter's ability to take on new ideas and products, but ultimately they are driven by a strong sense of practicality. They know that many of these newfangled ideas end up as passing fads, so they are content to wait and see how other people are benefiting before they buy in themselves. Furthermore, they want to see well-established references before making substantial investments. Because there are so many people in this segment (roughly one-third of the population), winning their business is key to any substantial profits and growth.

- **Late Majority**—This group is as practical as the early majority, but with one major difference. Whereas people in the early majority are comfortable with their ability to handle something new should they finally decide to purchase it, members of the late majority are not. As a result, they will wait to buy until a product or service becomes an established standard. Even then, they want to know that the product is well supported. This is one of the reasons they tend to buy from large, well-established companies. Like the early majority, this group comprises about one-third of the total buying population in any given segment. This group can be highly profitable, indeed, for while profit margins decrease as products mature, so do the selling costs and virtually all the R&D costs have been amortized.

- **Late Adopters**—These people resist new things, for a variety of reasons, some personal and some economic. The only time they ever buy something new is when it is buried so deep inside another product that they don't even know it is there (e.g., the way microprocessors are built into just about everything, including your refrigerator and your car, these days).

So what does this have to do with the hybrid sales channel? More importantly, how does this generic information help me *sell more* of *anything?* Let's make the answer every bit as simple as the description of the product life cycle curve:

Depending on where customers are on the curve and on where your products and solutions are on the curve, customers expect different levels of sales and support. To match the right sales coverage to the right circumstances you need to match the right resource, with the right capabilities, to where the customer and the product align on the curve. The right coverage can give you significant advantages, while the wrong match can doom your results.

For now, we're going to focus on the easy work of understanding how customers think, view, and react to products during their life cycles. At this point, all we're going to do is plot and document where each of the products and solutions you represent are on the curve today. That's it. To add some depth that will help you plan your hybrid sales channel coverage, we'll then add a distinction for each product or solution: Is that product primarily sold through your own direct sales efforts, through existing channel partners, or through both? In the end, both of these factors will help pull together the final plan.

Here's an illustration of what this looks like:

	STAGE	DIRECT	PARTNER
PRODUCT 1	INNOVATE	X	
PRODUCT 2	E MAJORITY		X
PRODUCT 3	L MAJORITY		X
PRODUCT 4	E ADOPTER	X	X

Seems easy enough, right? You can't know how to get to where you're going unless you know your starting point. From a product point of view, this will map out your starting point.

Identify which products your customers buy that "wraparound" your products to create a total solution to their needs and from whom they are buying those products and/or their total solutions.

When Jasmine and John were first working their way through the cocktail napkin, Jasmine didn't dare use any formal language like "whole product." That would have made the task seem harder than it already did. But, if you'll remember back to our ChannelPRO™ model discussion, "wraparound" is the concept of the whole product. This is the critical, and final, step of data gathering for building out your hybrid sales channel coverage model. It's another layer of keeping the customer at the core by looking at how they buy not just your product, but also at how they buy the whole product that solves their problem or meets their need.

Jasmine's cocktail napkin had room for the bell curve but could only represent whole product concepts down to the words "wraparound" with some arrows. We can do better than that on a slightly larger cocktail napkin here:

Just like the previous exercise, we should start with the customer's view before thinking about our own internal company view. What do you think is a key driving force behind channel sales having moved about 10 percent of many companies' revenues 25 years ago to more than 70 percent in many industries today? Some might suggest that it is an internal view, with companies trying to sell through lower-cost models. More accurately, it reflects how customers are demonstrating their buying preference: *Customers are seldom satisfied that a single vendor can put together all of the pieces of value that will solve their **whole** need. They turn to partners who can be more holistic in providing a total solution—a **whole product**.*

The whole product concept simply acknowledges that neither end users nor partners purchase only a product. "Whole product" refers to the totality of products, services, attributes, and partnerships that are required to completely meet end-user requirements throughout their buying process.

Partners contribute vital components of the whole product solution. Sometimes they contribute very tangible components such as physical equipment, software, or services, but they may also contribute less tangible elements such as local presence and knowledge or expertise in an industry.

Here's the point. Understanding what other pieces of the whole product your customers buy can help you leverage both your capabilities as well as those of your partners. You need not perform this analysis for all of the products and services you sell, but it should be done for those that are key contributors to your quota.

Looking at your coverage this way forces you into the customers' shoes. You'll need to understand how they will solve the business problems in front of them—or capitalize on the opportunities they are tasked to seize. Armed with this information and an analysis that includes your company's existing partners, you increase your odds of igniting revenue growth through your coverage plan. Planning will cease to be about how many of your products you can sell to whom and by when.

The final planning template in this chapter can be used to look at the whole product characteristics of any one product or service in your portfolio. For this product, you catalog the additional pieces of the solution that your customers typically buy and identify which of your partner firms are currently delivering the value elements associated with that product.

COMPONENT	PARTNER 1	PARTNER 2	PARTNER 3	PARTNER 4
PRODUCTS	X	X		
SERVICES	X		X	X
INTEGRATION	X		X	
LOCATION		X		X

Wrapping It Up: No More Templates Please!

Not everyone will use the same tools the same way when developing their hybrid sales channel. Each company will have its own characteristics and nuances that will cause them to morph these basic approaches to match their market conditions. What you have so far is a systematic way to think about how you will build a different kind of coverage strategy and to begin to act on it. You have some simple tools and concepts to use that should make doing the hard work a little easier. It can't be completely prescriptive because "one size doesn't fit all." Which brings us to the topic of the next chapter: What do we do next, after we have all this analysis done?

CHAPTER EIGHT

Putting It All Together—*The Hybrid Sales Channel Coverage Model*

t's time to put it all together. Now that you and the members of your entire team have finished the hard work, let's recap what you've accomplished so far:

☐ You understand the importance of keeping the customer at the core of your decisions, no matter how strong the internal forces that push you to make coverage decisions for other reasons.

☐ You understand the basic driver behind the business case: More coverage equals more growth.

☐ You've considered how to customize your coverage model to match the type of territory you have (single/large account, industry/vertical, geographic).

☐ You're focused on the three key areas of selling—creating opportunities, managing opportunities, and managing relationships—and plan to leave all other parts of what it takes to run a hybrid sales channel to others: channel managers, sales operations, channel marketing, or whomever you need to call on for support.

☐ You've been introduced to a systematic view of what it takes to run an entire channel business as represented by the ChannelPRO™ model. You understand how it can help you avoid turning the direct sales team into channel managers. You see the importance of the elements and how they link to your role as an overall territory general manager.

☐ You know you need to build coverage by partnering with channel sales professionals at the individual level, not managing at the channel partner firm level.

☐ You've started your analysis of how customers in your territory are currently buying, and you understand why it is more important to consider how they are buying than how you and others are selling.

☐ You've taken an inventory of your company's current business partners that are already selling into your territory so that you know "who is where" and "who knows whom." You've started to form a picture of their unique strengths versus yours.

☐ You've plotted your products and services on the product life cycle to give you perspective on the best coverage strategy based on the customer/product/channel fit.

☐ And finally, you've considered the effect that "wraparound" or whole product considerations have on how you might create your coverage model. You understand that your customer buys a full solution, not just your company's product components, and that how you cover your territory with the right partner sales professionals could give you great competitive leverage.

Equally important, you've learned the essential lesson of the seagulls. When constructing your coverage model, your hybrid sales channel, the most important guiding principle is the one taught by the seagulls. If you start with an attitude of "mine"—an attitude that says, "I alone can do it. I alone create the greatest value at the most important leverage points of my territory"—you'll get stuck with your beak in the sail while your customer flies away.

The ChannelPRO model we worked through in Chapter Six gives you the basics for a territory-level view of both market mapping and whole product. While you don't want to turn direct sales professionals into channel managers, you can still follow the systematic methodology to ensure you cover all of the bases as you bring our hybrid sales channel to life. The next stop around the circle is partner selection. In this case, we need to back up a bit before you can start selecting the partner sales professionals you'll need to make that $2 million.

Start by Identifying Your Direct Sales' Unique Strengths

There's a simple and sometimes humbling way to prevent seagull behavior when you start to build your hybrid sales channel—*keep the customer at the core*. After all, who is the best judge of what is "unique" in terms of a selling strength? You? Your product marketing team? Your boss or senior leadership?

The best and only true judge of a strength that will make a difference in sales success is the customer. If we go back to the basic concepts of their original text, *Strategic Selling*, that Bob Miller and Steve Heiman outlined, it's this simple:

> *To us, it makes no sense to say that a given product, service or solution is objectively better than another. Whatever you are proposing to your customer, it*

creates advantage only when the customer sees it that way—when she perceives the value that you're bringing to her business.

This same concept applies to an individual sales representative. It is what Henri had in mind when he wrote his second bullet on the whiteboard: Focus direct reps where they have unique strengths.

Before putting pen to paper to sketch out your unique strengths, we need to discuss a couple of criteria for deciding whether something is or is not a unique strength. These criteria are modified in their application from the more recent *The New Strategic Selling*:

1. **A Strength Is an Area of Differentiation**

   ". . . it enables the customer or prospect to identify a difference . . . you have a Strength only if this matters to your customer." If it doesn't *make a difference* to your customer, it is not a unique strength.

2. **A Strength Improves Your Position**

   "The use of a Strength increases your chances for success in the immediate sales objective for which you're setting a strategy . . . 'position' is just another term for strategy, and the point of strategy is to help you understand where you are, so you can take steps to move yourself and your company toward the close."

Isn't this the purpose of the coverage strategy you have in mind? To improve your position, you need to align your unique strengths with those of your partner sales professionals in a way that will improve your overall position.

The difference is that you're taking a broader view than just an immediate single sales objective when aligning strengths to a coverage strategy. Nevertheless, the criteria are likely to be more, not less, valid.

You now have all of the tools you need to do the work, but there is no standard template going forward. The format and outcome will look different for each of you. Your company, territory, and partner dynamics simply insert too many variables to allow us to apply a cookie-cutter approach.

Start by identifying your unique strengths. They will guide you to where you can create leverage and where you can add partner strengths to create additional leverage.

As a quick reminder, your unique strengths should fall into areas of:

- Specific accounts, departments, or functions within your territory
- Buying influences where you have specific value in their eyes (by name, title, or role)
- Industries, industry segments, or applications

- The value you, your company, and your partners add based on the product's life cycle stage

If you're John, can you identify enough unique strengths coverage to hit your $5 million of your $7 million quota?

Don't Just "Fill the Holes"—Find the Unique Strengths of Your Partners

The most common mistake, and a symptom of seagull behavior, is to use the analysis of your unique strengths to "lock in" on what will be covered by direct sales resources. This happens when you map out the places where you want to sell (with self-biased judgment) and use partner selection to fill the gaps in coverage. Doing this can get you accused of "cherry picking" opportunities—something your partners probably already think you do. The last thing you want to do is to prove them right.

There are several more reasons why this kind of early prejudgment can be flawed and could create a solution doomed to failure:

- It assumes that direct coverage is "better" than partner-based coverage, and you can end up looking for partners to fill gaps rather than capitalizing on their unique strengths as equal partners.

- It doesn't keep the customer at the core. It predisposes a solution.
- It risks alienating the partner sales professionals you approach to be part of the team. Intentional or not, it may appear to them that you are treating them as a lower class of sales resource, or at least that they are considered secondarily when planning for success "jointly".

It doesn't hurt to take what you *believe* the partners' unique strengths are, including where they are selling now, their relationships, their product and support strengths, and their whole product capabilities, and use those as your starting point. It is only a starting point, however.

You need to combine your judgment with a broader set of input to not only create the partner selection criteria, but also to actually select the partners themselves. Your data and all subsequent judgments need to be validated by the partners you target as candidates for your hybrid team. You may have already validated your conclusions with your channel managers or channel marketing team, but now it's time to have conversations with the actual individuals who may become your teammates. Understanding their knowledge and experience is crucial to ensuring you make the best selections possible.

If you know a particular partner well, your discussion may start out with the same kind of cocktail napkin conversation

Jasmine had with John. If you don't, it may require a more formal introduction through the channel manager assigned to the partner. You may also need to ask the channel manager to help you set up a joint meeting with the senior leadership of the firm.

How Ready Are They to Partner with You—and You with Them?

Setting criteria, having conversations, validating assumptions, and selecting partners for your territory doesn't end with the partner selection stage of our ChannelPRO model. It bridges over to the next section of the model, partner enablement. One of your key discussion points and a critical evaluation and selection criteria will be their readiness to do the job.

If you've only added partner sales professionals who are already selling into your territory, you might ask how they could possibly be "less than ready" to partner with you in a hybrid model. They might even take offense should you suggest such a thing. Remember, one of the first rules of dealing with partners: They run their own business and do things for their reasons, not yours. Who are you to judge a partner as "not ready"? They have just as much right to question your readiness to partner with *them*!

In the next chapter, we'll talk in more detail about how you can use the following figure to do a financial analysis and ROI justification for your hybrid sales channel project. It describes many of the actual sales and support activities that need to be performed every day in order for your customers to be successful. These activities are the customer-facing actions, whether done by the direct sales professional or the partner, that drive revenue and profit.

DIRECT SALES TEAM

- Demand-generation marketing
- Opportunity identification and qualification
- Discovery and solution creation
- Demonstration, pilot, proof of concept
- Proposal and commercial agreement creation
- Account coverage and relationship management
- Implementation planning and management
- Technical implementation
- Solution integration with customer systems or processes
- Postimplementation support

PARTNER SALES TEAM

Think of these as the "practical" enablement criteria that need to be applied to all parties in a hybrid model. They may be different than the capabilities your channel management and partner enablement teams currently focus on, but they are the critical enablement requirements to be identified, clarified, and in many cases, put into a territory agreement or territory plan. They also describe "who does what." This can help you eliminate redundancy in your customer-facing sales activities.

It is critical that you work with your targeted partners and the enablement teams in your organization and theirs when you determine who will be responsible for each of these activities. You may have partners that have superb unique strengths, yet fall short of being good candidates for hybrid territory partners based on their ability and willingness to:

- Honestly and openly discuss and assess their capabilities
- Build, stay committed to, and measure progress against plans
- Understand the benefits and costs of shifting these capabilities from one party to the other

Of course, no partner is going to fit perfectly into the jigsaw puzzle that you're building. However, open, honest assessment and fair and equitable treatment of each other by both parties is essential. In today's world, you will find there are places where you need to compete and others where you can partner. The only thing that you can't do is build avoidable conflict in the plan from the start.

Making Your Partner Program Work to Your Mutual Advantage

We've all met them. They come with many titles: *comp plan lawyers, partner plan wizards,* and so on. These lawyers and wizards spend an inordinate amount of time ensuring they leverage every possible way the plan can work to their advantage.

Who wouldn't? In the world of sales, where cash is king, we all pay close attention to the agreements, documents, and handshakes that define how we are going to make money!

However, there is a nuance that comes into play when thinking about comp plans from the perspective of a hybrid sales channel. Your direct sales compensation plan and your company's partner plan may have conflicting goals, objectives, payout, and leverage elements. When you bring these two sales energies together and ask them to work toward a common goal, the way they make money can get in the way.

As I mentioned at the beginning, this book was not designed as a solution to resolve conflict over compensation between channels. There isn't a "one-size-fits-all" prescription for compensation alignment between direct and indirect sales professionals in a hybrid model. There are simply too many industries, markets, business models, partner types, strategies, etc., to generalize about a solution.

What we can do is look at the existing direct sales compensation and partner plan elements and identify:

* Where are the opportunities for leveraging both plans so resources are aligned for the most effective coverage?
* What potential changes need to be made in either plan to overcome any immediately conflicting elements to prevent them from arising from the outset?
* Can you isolate any necessary changes to the markets where you plan to deploy a hybrid sales channel without creating friction in the markets where you do not?
* How will you handle partner firms who have a presence in territories where you decide to deploy a hybrid, yet cover other areas where they have sales resources that will not be subject to your initial hybrid deployment?
* How can you structure compensation elements, both financial and nonfinancial, in a way that will motivate and reward "quick wins" during the early rollout of the model, while building sustainability for the long run?

There are more questions than these, to be sure, and we'll outline the most critical compensation elements in Chapter Nine. However, as you plan your implementation, answering these basic questions up front will put you ahead of the game and give you a strong start toward your goal of igniting growth.

Measure Less, But Measure What You *Can* Measure

It's time to extend into a broader team discussion and pull together more resources than just the field sales team—we need to pull in finance, sales operations, and partner operations. You can't execute your plan for a hybrid sales channel without a good understanding of what you're going to measure from the start. We'll set some broad guidelines here and dig in deeper in Chapter Nine.

You may recall that the final picture of Jasmine's napkin included four important words: *Plan, Manage, Measure, Adjust.*

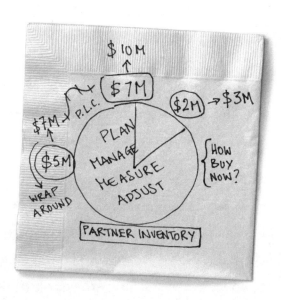

She knew that as soon as she put this model in place it would be under watchful scrutiny by senior-level leadership and that it needed to produce measurable, verifiable results. She also knew that partners would never buy into the model unless they understood which key metrics affected their own firm's performance. Finally, while growth was the key strategic objective, she knew that there would need to be leading metrics that would show the way and allow for quick course corrections along the way.

The overview of ChannelPRO in our discussion on sales productivity provided the backdrop and basic criteria for setting metrics for The Hybrid Sales Channel. They need to be practical, actionable, and mutually agreed upon. If you use these basic guidelines, follow the principle of "measure less, but measure what you *can* measure," and maintain a balance of leading metrics and trailing metrics, you'll have a pretty good idea of the kinds of metrics you need to add to your program.

Now, how do you sort out your metrics and put them into use?

1. Identify behavioral metrics that both you and your partners can agree on. At first, these may be as simple as executing your communication plan, meeting

agreed milestones, and sticking to the management review cadence you set up.

2. Initially, use financial metrics that are tied to the sales funnel, not closed business. Funnel health and velocity are far more important in the early stages of your program than quick wins. The latter may have been close to closing with or without your hybrid model.

3. Don't make metrics solely the responsibility of the direct and partner sales professionals. What do you expect from management? What commitments have been made by support functions and organizations? Can you tie these expectations and commitments to leading behavioral metrics that make success everyone's responsibility?

4. What baselines have you established against which you will measure growth? Are you aligned, up and down your business, on what the baseline is, what the target is, and what the time frames are? Do you have similar alignment between yourselves and your partners in each hybrid territory? Without alignment on the targets, you'll never agree on what success looks like.

5. How will you adjust if there appear to be predictive metrics that point to course corrections? How frequently should each metric be measured? What

is the source and reliability of the data? What is the management process for evaluating the metrics and making the necessary course corrections?

These last topics raise two essential questions:

1. How do we pay for this fundamental shift in our model?
2. How will we know if it is working?

So far, we've barely touched on these, but we'll get much more granular in the next chapter.

The Devil Is in the Details

We've already covered many major aspects of building the hybrid sales channel at a high level. However, the success or failure of the hybrid sales channel often comes down to how thoroughly you've thought through the details. If you overlook something on the internal organizational side, you could find your hybrid channel efforts lacking the critical support they need. If you miss something that is important to partners, they might end up concluding that this is just another sales strategy du jour and can't be bothered.

Below are a few things we see vendor organizations frequently overlook as they construct their hybrid channel.

These details run the spectrum from aspects the board or sales leadership needs to consider all the way down to questions that need to be answered by John as he builds his team. While this is not a comprehensive list of details, it should be enough to start you thinking in the right direction.

Your business model, current partner programs, corporate culture, and your unique style will all affect the details in your answers. When it comes to avoiding bumps in the road, sometimes taking the time to think through your answers can be more important than *how* you answer them.

- **Do you have executive sponsorship?** Change initiatives rarely succeed without executive-level sponsorship, and moving to a hybrid channel involves plenty of change. You might have to build their support through a pilot program, but wait until you have unquestioning support before rolling out the program more broadly.
- **Do you have channel manager buy-in?** So far, we've focused almost exclusively on John's point of view because he has the most work to do. Nevertheless, your channel managers need to understand how their roles and performance expectations are affected by the change.
- **Who else will you need to enlist?** If execution requires support from others in the organization, they will need

to understand what is expected of them. (This is one of those times where your executive sponsorship might come in handy.) For example, enablement may need to tweak their content and training programs to make them suitable for the hybrid sales professional.

- **How will you recognize performance?** Knowing that salespeople are motivated by recognition, you probably have a slew of yearly awards. Will the hybrid channel program change the qualifications for those programs or will you need to set up new categories? Is there a way to expand recognition to channel sales professionals in your hybrid channel, maybe even by making them eligible for a President's Club?

- **Will you offer exclusivity?** It's a question partners will almost always ask when a new program is rolled out.

- **Will you require exclusivity?** Remember, you're enlisting individual channel sales professionals, not entire partner organizations. While you may not require it, those channel sales professionals you select are very likely to be exclusive to near-exclusive by nature. Success will make them even more so.

- **Whose responsibility is it to address deficiencies in channel sales professional capabilities?** Sometimes channel sales professionals will oversell themselves, but it's not always serious enough to warrant throwing them off the team. For example, perhaps a channel sales professional's unique strength was supposed to be demand generation, but they aren't fulfilling their end of the bargain because they aren't getting the support of their marketing team. Is it the job of the channel manager or the territory manager to address this with them? When you think this through, it can help to consider the discussion we just had on enablement earlier in this chapter. How can you best address this potential issue, without turning a direct salesperson into a channel manager?

- **Do you have an exit strategy/process?** If a channel sales professional isn't living up to his or her end of the bargain, do you have a plan to dissolve the relationship? As with internal employees, having a well-defined process can make status changes easier on everyone.

- **What happens when a channel sales professional moves to a new organization?** Will he or she be grandfathered into the program automatically? Or will that person have to go through a probationary period to see if their new organization provides the same level of support?

- **How will your market development fund (MDF) program be affected?** If you offer an MDF, will it still be calculated and applied the same way? Or would it make more sense to treat marketing in the hybrid sales channel differently?

- **How will you manage the funnel?** Visibility into the channel funnel has always been an issue for channel organizations. However, hybrid channel sales professionals will be working much more closely with your territory managers. Maybe it's reasonable to expect them to use the same sales force automation system as your territory managers to remove a lot of the time and guesswork from producing forecasts. Thanks to software as a service, it is easy and relatively inexpensive to provide CRM/SFA access to an individual sales rep.

- **How can you minimize the impact of channel conflict?** Depending on your coverage model, you could have more than one channel partner in a specific account. Are there ways you can minimize conflict to provide the best experience possible for the customer? We touched on this earlier, but a key selection criterion for the hybrid channel sales professional may be his or her ability to work well with other partners.

- **What will you tell other channel partners?** Partners talk (brag?) to each other. While you may decide not to announce the program until it's proven successful, you need to be prepared to tell partners something in response to their questions as soon as you enlist your first channel sales professional in the pilot program. Before you roll out the program more broadly, you'll need to refine your messaging to avoid channel disruption as much as possible.

We're closing in on the finish with two stops left on our journey: How do we measure and pay for the business model (Henri may be focused on growth, but he does care about the numbers), and what kind of leadership model does it take to make this kind of change take place as well as to make the change *stick and last?* Stick with it to the finish, and you'll have what you need to build the case for your own Hybrid Sales Channel!

CHAPTER NINE

Measuring and Paying for the Hybrid Sales Channel

Despite Henri's dismay (bordering on disbelief), both Dominique and Jorge had given him relatively free rein to focus on growth over cost. The crux of the hybrid sales model is based on igniting growth, and growth creates money to pay for all sorts of new costs or expenses, especially when the growth is purely organic. Unfortunately, most of us do not have a C-Suite level strategic initiative or mandate to back this kind of a change. Many of you reading this book have the kind of critical finance team that we talked about earlier. These finance professionals view partner commissions as an expense, scrutinize duplicate commissions or costs, and work to maximize the most cost-efficient routes to market. They will have one question, and they will demand an answer: How will we pay for the hybrid sales channel?

The Key Is in the Coverage Model Itself

Do you remember the opportunities that Dominique laid out following the board's insistence on organic growth?

The magic is in the third bullet—aligning resource to opportunity. We've already talked about reducing duplicating selling actions by aligning unique strengths between direct and indirect resources in a hybrid mode. While this will absolutely create growth once fully developed, deployed, enabled, and reinforced, most of our finance teams are as hesitant to bet on "growth" as they are to fund current expenditures based on promises of future "productivity."

The key to convincing the most skeptical finance executive is to focus the math on execution, not results. Since finance people are cost-oriented creatures, it's an argument they should readily relate to. But, since most sales leaders are focused on results, let's walk through the math so you're prepared to present the business case.

Look back at the list of typical customer-facing marketing, sales, and support activities we just talked about in the last chapter:

- Demand-generation marketing
- Opportunity identification and qualification
- Discovery and solution creation
- Demonstration, pilot, proof of concept
- Proposal and commercial agreement creation
- Account coverage and relationship management
- Implementation planning and management
- Technical implementation
- Solution integration with customer systems or processes
- Postimplementation support

Each of these activities has a cost associated with it in addition to the value it creates for the customer. When Dominique talked about market coverage, she may not have been thinking about it at this level of granularity. However, when it comes to aligning resources to their greatest unique strengths, there are two truths we must remember: (1) costs follow resources, and (2) you can only afford to align the right resource to the right market opportunity if you ensure that no two resources are performing the same task.

This elimination of duplicate work creates the leverage that ignites growth, but it is the cost transfer between vendor and partner (and vice versa) that makes the math behind the funding model work. Failure to look at costs this way has doomed the financials of many partner programs from the start.

What do partner programs, doomed or not, have to do with funding this kind of shift in a market coverage model? Our history with them goes to the core of the point.

- Revenue is the cornerstone of many partner programs. The more revenue, the more preferential the pricing, resources, head count, programs, and access to discrete specialized skills provided to the partner. Revenue is king.
- More evolved, mature partner programs have moved to (or at the least, added) another basis for recognizing partner value and assigning "tier" benefits. *The partner's demonstrated ability to take on responsibilities and activities (a.k.a. costs and the ability to directly deliver value) that would normally be incurred by the vendor.*

We all have experience with the outcomes the first kind of partner programs produce. Our best partners may produce the most revenue, but they may also increase our costs due to their dependence on many aspects of our sales or support capabilities. Cost increases can be exacerbated by compensation systems that pay both direct and partner commissions on some or all sales. In any case, when we go about setting up a hybrid sales channel *purposefully* (as opposed to by default through our policies and practices), we should avoid the lessons already learned through our standard partner programs.

Fortunately, we're not looking at revamping an entire channel program when we implement a hybrid sales channel. You may decide your program needs alteration to accommodate the kinds of changes you plan to make, but remember, our hybrid channel sales program only affects specific channel sales professionals, not the entire channel partner firm. When we look at the financial implications of the hybrid sales channel, we need to look at the impact on costs, behaviors, resources, and customer value at the closest possible point to the customer—in each individual sales territory.

We're striving for a model that lets you examine each hybrid territory across a common set of criteria, as seen in the following image.

DIRECT SALES TEAM

- Demand-generation marketing
- Opportunity identification and qualification
- Discovery and solution creation
- Demonstration, pilot, proof of concept
- Proposal and commercial agreement creation
- Account coverage and relationship management
- Implementation planning and management
- Technical implementation
- Solution integration with customer systems or processes
- Postimplementation support

PARTNER SALES TEAM

To be customer-effective (as well as cost-effective), John and Jasmine need to be very transparent with the individual partner sales professionals who are candidates to join the hybrid sales team. These sales professionals need to know that they will be expected to act with as much independence as possible. John and Jasmine will also need to define, partner by partner, where they will back up the channel sales professional with resources or processes to support capabilities the specific partner candidate lacks.

This gives new meaning to the ChannelPRO™ process of partner selection. It demonstrates that there can be both growth and productivity improvement as well as cost reduction by infusing the direct sales territories with well-chosen partner sales professionals. Beyond all of the criteria that we discussed regarding relationships, industry knowledge, geography, whole product coverage, and product life cycle, we've now introduced the concept of partner self-sufficiency (or at least increased independence) as a key selection criterion for the hybrid sales channel team.

When you're able to solve this puzzle, the math works:

Increased Direct Sales & Support Team Productivity
+
Increased Growth Potential from Increased Direct
Sales Focus
+
Increased Sales Resource Coverage from Channel
Sales Partners
+
Increased Growth Potential from Alignment of Resource to
Greatest Unique Strengths
=
Higher Growth and Lower-Cost Sales Engine

Paying for Activity

If John is like every other sales professional on Earth—and he is—at some point he is going to ask the $2 million question: "Will I be paid on the entire $7 million or only on my $5 million?"

In the unlikely event that John doesn't ask, the CFO will. No CFO or board of directors likes the idea of paying double commissions, and compensation is one of those sticking points that can easily sink your business case for a hybrid sales channel if you're not prepared to address it.

Jasmine knows that part of the reason John is so successful is because he's motivated by his compensation plan. Plus, John is already sensitive about not being turned into a channel manager, and Jasmine knows she won't get his complete buy-in if he doesn't see a quick return for his efforts. She also knows that several of her fiercest competitors have been after John for years. If they sense John is unhappy about the new hybrid channel, they will smell blood in the water.

On the other hand, as we just discussed, the hybrid channel cannot work unless there is a cost transference. Even Jasmine's board of directors won't ignore costs forever. John needs to choose partners who can quickly become self-sufficient in executing the activities for which they are responsible. And, of course, the partner margin structure needs to fairly compensate partners for their activities.

While paying partners for their activities, Jasmine also needs to be certain John is fairly compensated for the activities for which he is responsible. So how should the organization structure John's compensation plan so that they aren't paying twice for the same activities, yet are incenting the right behaviors in their direct sales force?

Now and Forever

While compensation plans are designed to fairly compensate salespeople for their efforts, their structure is almost always designed to incent certain behaviors. The key for most organizations is to decide what sort of compensation plan makes sense now as they are looking to ignite the hybrid sales channel versus what makes sense down the road after the hybrid channel has been established.

Now

Although Jasmine has assured John he will not be turned into a channel manager, they both agreed they had plenty of work to do: building out the market model, finding the right partners, bringing them up to speed, and developing a communication/management cadence for the territory.

To ignite enthusiasm for the hybrid sales channel, you'll want to construct a compensation plan that pays the direct sales professionals for these efforts and incents them to do them well. However, we also need to think back to our earlier discussion of how important it is to avoid assigning basic channel enablement activities to the direct team.

Those responsibilities belong to the channel manager, and paying direct sales team members to do them would be paying twice for the same activity.

Forever

Although one of John's initial responsibilities is to select partner sales professionals who can be self-sufficient, there are some new responsibilities that will never go away, such as:

* Ensuring market coverage
* Coaching his chosen partner professionals
* Keeping customers at the core
* Forecasting

Let's examine each of these so that we can be sure it adheres to the key principle of not turning John into a channel manager:

* **Ensuring Market Coverage**—Market opportunities are dynamic. Territories change. Partners come and go. The hybrid sales channel is not one that is ever completely *finished*. The direct sales "general manager" will need to continue to complete activities like market mapping and partner selection once a year, if not more often, to ensure the right team is in place.
* **Coaching Chosen Partner Professionals**—While not managing partners as a direct sales team, there is time

to be spent coaching partners on the sales methodologies that have been proven successful. If the right partners have been chosen based on unique strengths, this is not a one-way street. The hybrid territory manager may receive just as much input from the channel sales professionals about what works and what doesn't in his or her territory.

- **Keeping Customers at the Core**—The hybrid sales channel is based on collaboration. John and his chosen partners will collaborate to ensure they are all using their unique skills to the greatest advantage. Since the team is made up of human beings, it's natural for different individuals to have different points of view, motivations, and approaches. It is critical to work hard to orchestrate these so that the customer remains at the core of all of their sales efforts.

- **Forecasting**—As the general manager for his territory, there is a new definition of the process of assembling the forecast. Although John is relying on his chosen partner sales professionals to bring in $2 million, the quota responsibility is still his. Sales leadership cannot wait until the year is over to see how the hybrid channel performed. For his own peace of mind (and career), he will want to know whether he's on track to reach his numbers.

No matter how self-sufficient the hybrid channel team is, these four activities will never go away. Much in the same way you would pay a sales manager a percentage of revenues, the direct sales team member needs to be compensated for these frontline activities.

How Will We Know If It's Working?

Ever heard the saying *the watched pot never boils*? That's what it can feel like if you sell the success of your hybrid sales channel on revenue only. Every month, if not every week, you'll have the CFO and the board asking what incremental revenues your new hybrid channel has brought in.

If your sales cycle is six months or longer, as many B2B complex sales cycles are, it can take some time for revenue to pick up even with channel sales professionals who are successfully selling your solutions already. That's why you need to focus initially on behaviors and activities (leading indicators) as you work to get your hybrid sales channel off the ground.

You may recall that the final picture of Jasmine's napkin included four important words: *Plan, Manage, Measure, Adjust*. The phases outlined below follow that process.

Phase 1: Plan

For the first few weeks, progress needs to be measured in terms of each individual's completion of the prerequisite activities. Has he created his market map and filled in the red flags? Has he chosen his partner sales professionals and ensured their buy-in? Does he have alignment with partner sales professionals on the activities for which they will be responsible and which responsibilities will fall to his organization? Has he set up a communication and opportunity management cadence with his chosen partner sales professionals?

How long this phase lasts can be a function of the maturity of your channel organization and the direct sales professional's understanding of his or her territory. As almost every organization we've worked with has discovered, you probably don't know as much as you think you know about your territory and who is selling to whom. It's important to do a thorough job of filling in the gaps in this phase, and you'd be wise not to rush it.

Phase 2: Manage

Phase 2 starts sooner for some channel professionals than for others, but this is where the rubber meets the road. They are now in the territory selling, but again, if the sales cycle is lengthy, it can take some time for revenues to increase.

Luckily, there are a number of leading indicators that can predict future success such as:

- New contacts made
- New opportunities identified
- New opportunities per sales stage

Phase 3: Measure

Of course, the ultimate leading indicator for each individual is going to be whether they are on track to meet their entire quota. From a broader perspective, however, there are several financial metrics that ought to make it to your list of Key Performance Indicators:

- **Customer Satisfaction**—This is a must-have metric, since the successful hybrid channel keeps the customer at the core. A drop in customer satisfaction is a leading indicator for trouble ahead and may be a signal that your hybrid sales channel is dysfunctional. Whether you have a sophisticated net promoter score (NPS) metric already in place or can quickly put something simple into place for those customers affected by the hybrid channel change, some level of measurement is critical.
- **Year-Over-Year Revenue Increase**—Depending on your business model and territory arrangement, you can slice and dice this metric several ways: customer, territory,

market segment, etc. Revenue is one of the primary ways organizations measure productivity, and since the goal of the hybrid sales channel is growth, this is the key metric that tells whether the program is working. If you measure your hybrid sales channel model effectively, you'll be able to get very granular over time as to not only *what* revenue increases—but *where, how, from whom,* and *why.*

- **New Customer Acquisition/Account Penetration**—From the beginning, the mandate has been organic growth. That means either the construction of a hybrid sales channel that can bring in new accounts, or one more broadly focused on increased account penetration, perhaps for specific product lines.

- **Channel vs. Direct Contribution**—Our focus is on overall pie growth, but we also want to look closely at the contribution percentages. As we established in Chapter One, all sales channels in John and Jasmine's organization were underperforming. However, John had made his numbers for the past five years. The channel wasn't discussed during the initial discussion between John and Jasmine. It didn't need to be. They both knew channel sales had been lackluster with very little organic growth. So if we look at the $7 million pie, the channel contribution should be a higher percentage than normal, while John's contribution as a percentage may actually drop.

The one time this indicator should set off alarm bells is when the contribution from direct sales rises as a percentage. It's not always a problem, but it can be a sign that John is treating direct as the preferred sales channel and making his or her numbers off the backs of the hybrid channel sales professionals. If this is the case, it needs to be addressed before irreparable damage is done to John's (and the organization's) reputation in the channel. Once trust is lost, it can be very hard to reestablish.

- **Overall Share of Customer Wallet**—In addition to driving growth of the total pie and creating organic growth, at the end of the day, you're also looking to grow the share of your customers' spending that flows to you rather than to other places. This is the most difficult measurement to make, especially if you don't have a system with data already flowing to establish a baseline before you begin.

Phase 4: Adjust

Certainly, you would expect to need to make adjustments in the early days, and perhaps after you pass significant milestones, e.g., six months, one year, etc. However . . .

Whatever It Was That Got You Where You Are Today Is Not Sufficient to Keep You There

Sales management is inherently a cycle: plan, manage, measure, and adjust. Even if your strategy is successful today, you never stop measuring. The hybrid sales channel is no different. In the beginning, very small but frequent course corrections will keep you on course. Large, infrequent course corrections disrupt the flow of business and will run your ship aground.

A few factors can help you define the cadence of your communications plan and measurement cycle at all levels of management:

- What small number of simple actions can you add to each layer of management so that quick monitoring and adjustment is practical and possible? How will you measure and ensure that they happen?
- How will you share information across the organization— especially with your partners—as to what is working and not working? How frequently? Using what media and methods?
- Most important, what will you *stop doing* to make time for the additional tasks that will come from the early phases of getting your hybrid sales channel off the ground?

CHAPTER TEN

Making Extraordinary Things Happen Through Company Alignment

We begin the end of our journey by returning to the beginning. As we talk about the final aspect of ChannelPRO™ to be applied in the creation of a hybrid sales channel, we have to start with company alignment. This starts at the top, but it's more than a matter of getting executive sponsorship. No matter what level of executive support you have for your hybrid sales channel, change like this doesn't happen from the bottom up. It takes execution *action* and inspired leadership.

Five Key Tenets of Effective Leadership

Before we dig into the many facets of company alignment, let me tell you a story from a time earlier in my career. Each of us has been inspired and encouraged by others to accomplish extraordinary things in our lifetime. Some lead and inspire by words, others by deeds, and some by the best combinations of both. One of the greatest sources of inspiration came midcareer from a senior executive I reported to three separate times—twice while at IBM and once while leading sales and marketing at a large communications solutions distribution company. David described himself as a "servant leader," and while that term may have come from a book he had read or an executive development program, he walked the walk.

In my second stint of working for him, we were in the middle of one of the greatest transformations in IBM's history. We had our first "outside" CEO and were shrinking head count by nearly 50 percent. At the same time, we were also trying to reposition ourselves from being a traditional hardware and software company to a visionary IT services firm. In a company of IBM's size and maturity, these kinds of changes require a level of alignment and leadership that is almost unimaginable. Some might argue to this day whether or not we were successful, but that's not the reason I'm telling you this story.

My experiences under David's leadership are particularly helpful in wrapping up our discussion of what it takes to ignite growth through a hybrid sales channel. Like Dominique, David was managing an organization through great change, and he needed to create a shared vision. In turn, we needed to provide leadership to our direct reports so that they also shared the same vision.

I wasn't aware of the source at the time, but David drove home five key tenets that are embossed in a piece of glass I still keep on my office bookshelf:

1. Model the Way
2. Inspire a Shared Vision
3. Challenge the Process
4. Enable Others to Act
5. Encourage the Heart

Later I learned that these were principles from the long-standing book on leadership, *The Leadership Challenge: How to Make Extraordinary Things Happen in Organizations* by James M. Kouzes and Barry Z. Posner.

Model the Way

When David infused these concepts inside of me, building them into my leadership DNA, he demonstrated his mastery of the first principle: **Model the Way**. He used actions, not words; deeds, not promises. David modeled this type of leadership, and I modeled him. I didn't have to read the book to understand what the principles meant. I just followed David's example.

As we've watched the executives, managers, and salespeople in our fictitious organization work through the many iterations of execution, measurement, financials, and more of The Hybrid Sales Channel, you might be thinking Dominique and Jorge were rather conspicuous by their absence. For instance, they did not insist on being present when Henri recruited Jasmine. Nor were they or Henri present when Jasmine enlisted John. You can bet none of them will insist on accompanying John when he meets with potential hybrid channel sales professionals. When you have company alignment, everyone is tuned to the same vision, and you don't need to oversee the execution personally.

So, how did Dominique, Jorge, Henri, Jasmine, and John provide leadership? By leveraging the five principles from Kouzes and Posner (as exemplified by my former boss, David). Let's look at each of these tenets in turn.

Dominique sets a fine example of **Model the Way**. Do you remember her first reaction to the board's ultimatum? What words would you use to describe her immediate frame of mind? Calm? Deliberate? Thoughtful? Certainly, terms like incendiary, reactionary, or emotional would not be included on that list. One could not blame Jorge for being slightly

impressed at Dominique's ability to set aside natural emotions, process the input, and create strong tenets for action.
How well would you have done?

This is the first example of the five leadership tenets, but
it isn't the last.

Inspire a Shared Vision

In swift succession, Dominque modeled the next principle:
Inspire a Shared Vision. The first shared vision had to be
between her and Jorge. They absolutely had to be on the same
page as to how to accomplish the board's directives. In doing
so, Dominique didn't settle for the status quo. Instead, she
even called out her own expertise and experience as potential
barriers to success. If you recall, she boldly wrote out her perspectives, the good and the bad, in black and white, as seen
in the following two images

OPPORTUNITIES FOR ORGANIC GROWTH

① ALL SALES CHANNELS UNDERPERFORMING

② MARKET COVERAGE

③ ALIGNMENT OF RESOURCE TO OPPORTUNITY

④ FOCUS ON GROWTH, NOT COST

> **OBSTACLES TO ORGANIC GROWTH**
>
> ① I'VE NEVER DONE IT
> ② YOU'VE NEVER DONE IT
> ③ NEW PRODUCT FUNNEL CAN'T HELP IN TIME
> ④ ALL SALES CHANNELS UNDERPERFORMING

Part of Dominique's initial genius was in bridging the inspiration of a shared vision to the challenges of actual execution. She identified the barriers that needed to be overcome and what she was personally willing to do to foster change. How many senior leaders have you met in your career who are as self-aware and willing to admit their own (and the company's) shortcomings in the face of adversity or a challenge? In her first reactions, you see the elements of what will become aligned leadership if she stays the course.

Challenge the Process

It takes a very special kind of leadership to begin an initiative by not only challenging existing processes and results, but challenging and questioning the very core circumstances that have brought people and companies to where they are. Leaders like Dominique, Jorge, and Henri aren't completely

rare species, but it is most often about what they *do next*—
rather than how they analyze what has occurred—that sets
the best apart from the rest.

Even John challenged the process, didn't he? He brought
critical thought and his experience to the table to ensure that
the "newfangled approach" was sound in the eyes of the customer. I encounter people all the time who apologize for being
blunt and direct with their input and how they feel about the
inadequacy about a given process, tool, or person's contribution. So long as they are being constructive and fact-based,
I'd far rather them be open and direct than let the status quo
go by, when clearly the best of the best are always seeking to
get better.

Creating a new coverage model like The Hybrid Sales
Channel will *by definition* challenge your existing processes,
assumptions, systems, and, perhaps, even cultural mores.
I was with a client recently via live video feed in a meeting of their sales team and all of their partners where they
fell directly on their sword about why the current coverage
model, behaviors, and resulting outcomes were not working—
for them and for their partners—and publicly committed to
change the way they do things in a Hybrid Sales Channel
approach. It is a bold move to challenge your own processes
in public with your partners! In their case, Cortez has indeed
burned the ships.

Enable Others to Act

The next inspired leadership element was equally critical: **Enable Others to Act**. It wasn't as simple as when Dominique called Henri and scheduled a meeting with him for the next day. That's simply line management command and control; it doesn't require much leadership skill. However, our story has several good examples of leaders enabling others to act.

Dominique cascaded her ability to build on a shared vision as she modeled her own version of leadership. She didn't dictate anything other than the strategy and board objectives when she reached out to her sales leader, Henri, letting him take the lead. At no time do we see her telling him what to do and how to do it. She enabled him to act, and in doing so, encouraged the same behavior as it played out in the next two key stages:

- Early on, Henri identified Jasmine as a first-line manager with the capacity to be a real change agent in the process. Then, he enabled her to act and gave her the necessary responsibility and accountability to do so.
- In turn, Jasmine homed in on a challenging but culturally visible individual contributor who, while a skeptic at the start, could be a galvanizing force for change by setting an example for his peers.

Before we talk about the last tenet, **Encourage the Heart,** let's talk a little bit about creating company alignment and a shared vision with channel partners. Remember, it's not just initial alignment that is important. The shared vision and alignment must be maintained all the way through implementation, management, measurement, and success.

However, because of the independent nature of channel partners, creating and maintaining a shared vision takes on an added degree of difficulty. Remember, they do things for their reasons, not yours. When your managers and direct sales professionals meet with individual partner sales professionals to talk about joining the hybrid team, their goal is to inspire a shared vision between the firms. Their leadership style and how well they follow the above tenets tells the partner a lot about whether this is another "programme du jour" (where the real goal is partner control) or a real change they should get behind.

Undoubtedly, you'll run into processes, both internal and external, that you'll need to challenge in order to be successful. Some will be financial; others operational Some of them will represent tradition, history, or old-school thinking about "how we've always done things around here." Resistance to change will help you identify those people who do not like change but who hold the key to processes that have to change in order for you to be successful.

For inspiration in working with these individuals, you might want to revisit the masterful way Jasmine built a shared vision (and mission) with John. It isn't as easy as following five seemingly simple tenets and then patting ourselves on the back as we congratulate ourselves on how aligned we are. *Everyone* has hard work to do before we start seeing results.

That's why we devoted Chapter Nine to leading behavioral metrics. While you want to enable people to act, you can't afford to wait for results to course correct. You must pay attention to what people are *doing,* and not just what they *say* they are doing. Being aligned, both internally and externally, is about measurable action on the core principles of a hybrid sales channel while building a framework to ensure that the entire initiative is set up for success. Set the foundation, build the vision, and then establish a leadership framework that is aligned, top to bottom, inside to out. Finally, let people do their job and hold them accountable for action.

Encourage the Heart

Now we've come to the last of the five leadership principles: **Encourage the Heart.** While last, it's critically important. As a leader at IBM, David had some remarkable traits: humble yet strong, self-aware *and* self-critical, willing to do what it took to support his team and make *us* successful, both as individuals and collectively.

Above all these, his skill in providing encouragement, praise, and recognition of a job well done was phenomenal. This didn't just come in the form of awards at our annual recognition events, although David went all out to make sure the "best of the best" knew who they were, what they had done right to get there, and why they were valued. He recognized performance every day and in every way you might imagine: a quick, unexpected comment in the hallway, a brief note when least expected, a story told to me about "something David said about you recently" . . . and on and on.

As leaders, you would think it would be easy for us to be good at the formal part of recognition and reward. We've spent our careers setting up formal systems that track trailing indicators and compensating (and being compensated) for them. Yet, myriads of consulting firms are in business purely because of our inability to do so *effectively* and *predictably*.

Despite the fact that many of these consulting firms promote themselves as being change management gurus, it's rare to find one that talks in terms of **Encouraging the Heart**. For the most part, it's all about the nuts and bolts of performance: setting the right metrics, assigning responsibility and accountability, establishing a management cadence, compensating for performance, and so on. In my opinion, they've forgotten one of the most important tools we have in getting people to change: the heart.

When making a hybrid sales channel part of your sales culture and eliminating seagull behavior, it's not just about *what you do,* but also about *how you do it.* You need to recognize and reward (immediately) the behaviors that a few will exhibit early but that you want all others to emulate. I see the leadership tenets as more of a circle than a list. You Model the Way when you Encourage the Heart. By showing people what success looks like and what you value, you will inspire them to seek it themselves.

Creating Company Alignment

Now, let's turn to the practical elements of company alignment: How do you do it? That depends on how misaligned you are. In some cases it can be as simple as we have seen depicted here—perfect people acting perfectly! Unfortunately, that's seldom the case. That's why we've stressed the hard work required since Chapter One. Aligning the company during the building and deployment of a hybrid sales channel typically takes several kinds of action steps:

1. Gather all sorts of current-state data about how direct and indirect sales are performing today. This includes near-term performance projections—essentially, how they are expected to perform if you don't transform

channel strategy. These data will help you build a shared vision of the need for change. Absent the opportunity for growth or the risk of serious trouble, few people will be motivated to make a major change in behavior.

2. Identify the existing corporate strategic initiatives that are in place or under way that would be affected by such a change. Determine the specific metrics of those initiatives and how the company is performing against them. How can you gain leverage by linking the hybrid sales channel to these initiatives? This step will help you connect the changes required of the hybrid sales channel to something that is highly visible and valued as a corporate strategy. When individuals can see how the hybrid sales channel can help them achieve their existing goals, the barriers to change come down quickly.

3. Build your hybrid strategy and tactics in alignment with company objectives from the start and include all of the key senior stakeholders it will take to make it successful. In our experience, this usually takes the form of a day-long face-to-face "workout" (to borrow a GE term) to review the case for change, build a plan for going forward, and get everyone aligned. All stakeholders must leave the room understanding their

role in the change and what they are going to be held accountable for.

4. Once leadership is aligned, and the hard analytical work has begun, it's time for a series of discussions with partners. There are two types of meetings you need to set up:

- Joint planning discussions at the principal level with key partner firms that may have multiple individual contributors worth recruiting at the territory level

- One-on-one, initially casual conversations between direct and channel sales professionals in the territory— much like the first conversation between Jasmine and John

- Both sets of discussions must be truly "joint" in nature so that the partners at both levels see and feel the opportunity to contribute, form, and shape the plan. Above all else, they must not be made to feel like the plan is being brought to them for execution as if they were an extension of your force of seagulls. *They are not.*

5. Select two small teams across levels and functions to monitor and manage the progress of the initiative. These teams will be instrumental in knocking down roadblocks to progress and providing resources quickly when needed.

- **Your Internal Team**—All of us have experience with steering committees or other types of teams that focus on the execution of important initiatives. The sad truth is that most of them don't perform very well because they look only at what is *not working* instead of focusing on what is working with an eye on replicating success and creating as many quick wins as possible. Your internal team needs to own the results of the hybrid sales channel, and one member of the team **must** be a senior executive who owns the results for the company. That person doesn't have to lead the team, but he or she must be visible, present, and active—and must not delegate his or her responsibilities. Disengaged senior executives are easy to spot: They habitually miss key meetings or get distracted by important/urgent issues during meetings. Note: The choice of the term *Executive Owner* instead of *Executive Sponsor* is deliberate. The difference between the two is self-explanatory.
- **The Joint Company and Partner Team**—This team needs to be equally small, but cross-functional and representative of every partner type that will be engaged at the territory level. The communication standard needs to include

an absolute encouragement of open, direct, and immediate feedback so that the hybrid sales channel can be viewed through the extended eyes of partners and employees. This will allow you to spot potential problems and opportunities and attend to them in a timely fashion.

6. Set up a communication and meeting cadence right from the start—and keep it. As time goes on, the communication plan becomes even more important. Why? As we've said before, employees and partners take their cues from leadership. If the case for change is sound, the opportunity for growth real, the strategy for avoiding pitfalls valid, then why don't we keep our commitments to communication and meetings (and to manage and measure) as the initiative gets past the initial stages? Because regardless of how transformative the hybrid sales channel can be, the reality is that most of us have a dozen or more "strategic" initiatives going at any one time. Plus, as simple as keeping our commitments sounds, we all know how hard old habits are to break. In this case, turning over a new leaf is vital to the success of the initiative.

I read a book several years ago after it caught my attention in an airport bookstore: *Made to Stick—Why Some Ideas*

Survive and Others Die by Chip and Dan Heath. The book had a strip of my favorite tool on the cover (duct tape!). I was pleased to find that it was just as insightful on the inside as it is clever on the outside.

The Heath brothers weave stories about an achievement that is rare in today's businesses—getting changes to stick. For any initiative to have the desired effects, change has to *actually take place*. They outline six principles that "maximize their stickiness" of new ideas. The final idea is to create "stories." That's what I still remember most about my time at IBM and the challenges we went through trying to make changes and get them to stick. I remember the stories we created to paint the picture of what success could look like.

What stories will you create to ensure your success? I look forward to hearing them as you tell us about your success in building your Hybrid Sales Channel!

Afterword
Where Do We Go from Here?

recognize that most of us do not go about taking on this kind of change as a completely Do It Yourself (DIY) project: Buy a book, internalize the principles, go make major change. Most often, individuals don't even consider taking actions that could put them at more risk than the opportunity for reward . . . unless they have credible, relevant experience with the person or firm who might guide or assist them in taking that action.

If your business conditions are such that there is either significant growth available, or trouble to avoid, by forming (or improving) some version of your own Hybrid Sales Channel—let me suggest some ways that we might help you down the path. Here are some examples of capabilities that our firm can bring to the table, some free and some fee, to add resources and best practices to making these Hybrid Sales Channel practices *your own* and not ours:

1. **Business Case for Change**

    This is typically a brief consulting engagement that includes a construct for informed discovery, diagnosis, and review of your current and desired future state, with outcomes designed to support your own creation of a business case for change at your company.

2. **Executive Alignment Around the Need to Change**
No project of this sort should begin without the creation and facilitation of a leadership workshop to align your key stakeholders (internally, externally, or both) around what it takes to make the change that your business case calls for. The outcomes include documented accountabilities, actions, timelines, metrics—and hopefully, actual alignment itself.

3. **Hybrid Sales Channel Readiness Assessment**
Whether you've built a case for change yet, or are looking to determine if you have the potential to actually "get to" your desired future state, we can help you do a simple assessment of your readiness to take on the change. The outcomes can be as dramatic as a go/no-go decision matrix, or as practical as an analysis of where the gaps are that need to be closed in order to make change happen *and stick.*

4. **Hybrid Sales Channel Management Workshop**
As you have seen, there is a lot of work ahead for the first-line managers and individual sales producers (both direct and indirect) who are going to create the actual working hybrid model. It's important to get

the managers aligned with what work is ahead, what the payoff is, and what tools will be available to them to help them drive the process as your own team of Jasmine look-alikes.

5. **Hybrid Sales Channel Concept Training**

Without taking your people out of the field to rally them to the task, how do you get your team trained in the concepts and tools necessary to create your own version of a Hybrid Sales Channel? We provide a series of electronic workshop modules that can help your team get up to speed quickly and productively.

6. **Hybrid Sales Channel Toolkit**

If only life were as simple as using some quick tables created on whiteboards as the tools to do your coverage strategy! From market mapping to whole product, partner selection, and more—we have an entire electronic toolkit that you can use to tailor to and support whatever version of a Hybrid Sales Channel makes sense for your company.

This isn't our first time around the block with these concepts, and I doubt it's all completely new to you either—but we're seriously capable with resources in every region of the world and speaking most every major language of business and culture on the planet. We're here, and we can help. If you'd like a better view, come by our web site dedicated to this concept, *www.thehybridsaleschannel.com.*

No need to have an impersonal marketing inbox. Write or call me directly—it's that important to me, to know what you want to accomplish. I look forward to hearing from you.

rich.blakeman@mhiglobal.com

+1 720.833.8706

Index

About Rich Blakeman

What matters to me is simple: help our clients and their clients solve problems and build consistent and long-term value. Improving the customer experience is at the core of what drives all of us in this business. We're here because the customer is what matters. This perspective, along with the best methodologies for effecting strong sales performance and an unprecedented team of thought leaders in channel sales, is what drove me to my current role leading the Channel Sales Center of Excellence for MHI Global. I enjoy the good fortune of being a regular keynote presenter on sales best practices for global companies across the sales advisory spectrum.

Throughout my 35 years in sales and marketing, I have been hands-on when it comes to motivating and building teams and interfacing with clients—resulting in consistent delivery of customer wins. I began my career at IBM, where I spent 19 years cultivating my skills in sales, marketing, and leading all facets of the customer experience. Through the years, I have facilitated many strategy and training workshops for clients across multiple industries—technology, telecommunications, healthcare, and other industries using diverse routes to market. As a senior executive, I have led sales and marketing for partner firms of industry leaders such as Oracle, Microsoft, Siemens, Cisco, and Lotus.

I just celebrated my 40th anniversary with my high school sweetheart, and we are the proud parents of two adult urbanites, one in San Francisco and one in Chicago.